Swaggerin' Beneath the Dublin Skies

Swaggerin' Beneath the DUBLIN Skies

Poems from IRELAND and Beyond
Plus Alaska 2000 (Travel Journal)

by
Frank Holt

GRATEFUL BED
PRESS

Dedicated to Eileen, whose champagne smile
swayed me towards the bubbles.

CONTENTS

About the Author

I was born in Dublin, Ireland in 1953.After 11 years working for the Irish railroad company the itchy feet syndrome touched my life. I landed in Boston in'82.Follwing a lengthy road trip I became a commercial fisherman in the Florida Keys. In '85 I moved to San Francisco where I met Eileen. Love blossomed immediately. We married in Dublin in '87. After a major earthquake I joined the San Francisco Painter's Union and worked precariously repairing the exterior of damaged high rises. In 2000 we relocated back to Ireland [via Alaska] and started a small bed and breakfast [called The Grateful Bed] in a beautiful little lakeside village called Ballyknockan in County Wicklow just 45 minutes from Dublin. Eileen is an accomplished artist who relished her years both in Ireland and Europe.

In 2011 we returned to America and landed in Portland, Oregon on the Pacific northwest. It's a truly wonderful town, drenched in free spirits, with a reputation for embracing dreamers.

Words have always accompanied my journey. Poetry is the breath of young life. The poems are an extension of my being, little gasps of fresh air. As the words seep through, a kind blessing engulfs me. When inspiration fades, I gaze at the stars and wait for silent whisperings.

Dublin Pub Scenario

With gob smacked anticipation
I plonk the arse down
The caress of derrière and aged mahogany
Calms the trembling of my breath
Just a silent nod
And he grabs the glass
The bend of an elbow
My life is in his hands.
Battered by the avalanche
Of banter draped in silk
I drown in the flood
Of a verbal symphony

He paws the amber stained apron
Grabs my pint
The Mona Lisa is mine
A mere arms length away
I momentarily resist
Admiring the foaming saviour
Slug
Followed by the familiar relief
Sigh
I trample over the edge
Of a world confused
By the threat of sobriety

Porters, ales and fairytales
Ghosts seeping through the cracks
Nooks and crannys
Stained-glass snugs
The harmony of humanity
A tavern's waltzing womb.
In the depths of a dimly lit corner
The fiddler flaunts his majesty
The songster airs an ancient myth
The poet steals the subtleties
Verses carved so silently
Weaving the rhythms of wisely words

Slug
The fusion of tangled thought
Sigh
Invitation to the blues
Smile
Shelter from the storm
I fling the eye around
Dublin untamed
The parade of pondering punters
Ploughing through the motions
Slug, slug, gone
Paddy
Nod!!!!

The Simple Man

And I a child
Soaked in laughter
Rampantly wide eyed
Untouched by need nor greed
Saw him gently kiss the rain
And laugh the hearty laugh
As croaking blackbirds cleansed
Within his pools of love touched muck.
All this in freedom
And unleashed solitude
Within his leafy stone walled world.

Seemingly alone
Tramping endlessly
'tween grey and verdant hills
In aged and tattered garbs
He smiled the silent smile
And glanced at dampened moss
Curling through stony crack 'n crevice.
He paused and lingered gazingly
As falling leaf swayed and swaggered
Merrily rafting towards raging foam
He sighed when the hidden moon
Teased four strong gusts
As willows weeped seductively
And the forest aired the ancient air.

Suddenly, I the child
Understood he was not alone
As butterflies tossed their golden wings
And mingling maggots ploughed the soil
In his world of endless song.
As sun light slumbered o'er the hills
He languished 'neath the quivering pines
The sparrow's frenzy ceased
Buzzing bees reposed
He bid the curtained sky adieu
As scented turf touched the clouds
And strolled towards fiery flames-a-waltzing
Leaving his world to the stars and me.

I fled and fled across oceans dark
And glanced through eyes of a different mind
Journeying through the wilderness
I saw the fear in children's eyes
And the maddening race of time against time
Yet I, with skin of childhood shed
Burdened with the endless search
Still seek the water's edge
Smile the silent smile
And dream of stony walls.

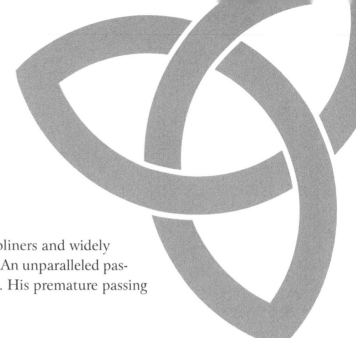

Preface-Luke Kelly

Luke Kelly was a founding member of The Dubliners and widely renowned as one of Ireland's finest folk singers. An unparalleled passion resonated from his voice. Wild to the core. His premature passing in 1983 still saddens the nation.

Eyes Shut Tight

(for Luke Kelly)

He sang of Raglan and rocky roads
Eyes shut tight, ginger head tilted back.
Like a towering inferno
Flaming mop alights the stage
Woven words pour forth
With a pulse ferocious and untamable

His voice the heartbeat of a nation
Soaked in the resonance of a Viking town
Verses soared with a venomous thrust
Tales of simplicity scorned and gaswork walls
Rebel man with a fiery tone
Chilling to the blood-drenched bone

I saw him rambling down the quays
In the 70's, full length fur coat
Disheveled as the weavings of a wintry gust.

Tempted to throw him a howaya
The child in me feared a response
Off I fled with the Liffey's flow

An enlightenment accompanied his gaze
A depth I longed to fly within
His weapon was the spoken word
Swaying with the wrath of a banjo's strings
And in his trembling interpretations
Songs took on life, soaring beyond human grasp.

Vices dragged him to his knees
Silencing the soul of a solemn city
He farewelled a hunger that begged for more
The bearded ones jammed beneath the steeple
Uileann pipes seeped through the sadness
An emptiness crawled through Dublin town
And in the wooden box
The whisperings of a restless ghost
Eyes shut tight.

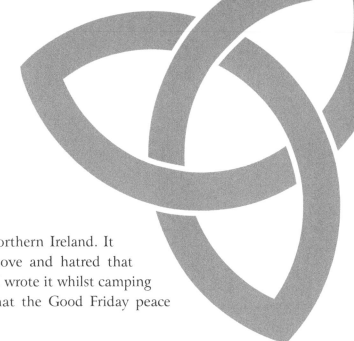

Preface-The Beauties Of Our Land

This Poem is simply a prayer for peace in Northern Ireland. It attempts to highlight simultaneous acts of love and hatred that occurred on a daily basis during the troubles. I wrote it whilst camping under the California stars the same week that the Good Friday peace agreement was being negotiated.

THE BEAUTIES OF OUR LAND

As howling torrents rage upon our western shore
A bullet pierces silence while northern rains still pour
A wide-eyed child observes with disillusioned grief
The horror of the moment paused in disbelief
A mother's broken heart must breath with wound unhealed
As Autumn leaves descend upon a distant field.

Upon the resplendent isle, a blind insouciance
Has squeezed the pulse of laughter from youthful innocence
The power hungry thieves who crossed our soothing sea
Have darkened darkened Rosaleen who weeps on bended knee
Yet from that lowered countenance towards the sky she glanced
Where feathered flight majestically sang and swayed and danced
Deep within the blue terrain roamed a restful cloud
Someday I'll share your freedom she passionately vowed.

Her spirit like a rose unfurled stretching towards the sky
Whispering o'er the famined soil your dream must never die

Upon the fading embers the sparks refused to yield
As pensively her soul lay bare upon that verdant field
The years of wretched turbulence have redefined our isle
Reposed upon the ocean's edge with eyes that calmly smile.

Fiery as a rampant horse our children's children grow
And stare upon the love and hate that seeds of madness sow
As wrinkled mirthful seanchai air an ancient myth
A youthful life is lain 'neath some cold and darkened pit
As the fiddler shares his gift inside the tavern door
A Belfast heartbeat leaps as hated sirens roar
As the Clareman ploughs the soil and glances at a cloud
A gunman treads alone towards an unassuming crowd.

In Donegal they resurrect the dying native tongue
As the splendor of our language flows from lives so young
Old Erin drenched in lamentation casts a mournful sigh
While peering contemplatively through weary emerald eye
The spirit of your people with the skylark shall reside
Whilst dignity and courage blossom by your side.

Before the bloody winds of rage release their ancient bind
The lessons from injustice gained must dwell within their mind
The powers of love and wisdom like morning dew must rise
And spread the scent of righteousness through narrow visioned eyes
The years of loss and suffering like youthfulness must fade
Then the restless pores of mind in peacefulness may bathe
Our hearts remain divided by a line across the sand
I pray someday our children share the beauties of our land.

AND STILL SHE SINGS

And still she sings
My feathered companion
Unsilenced by the harshness
Of a February hour
Untethered by shivering weathers
That weaken the mind of human kind.

    A frantic redbreast
    Darting like splattered blood
    Within the drenched shelter
    Of a wind-wrapped beech

She eyes all 'round
The readied robin
Throws me a wayward wink
Abandons all caution
Then plunges hastily
Towards the banquet in waiting

    The wee warrior
    Savouring the sumptuous seeds
    Slapped by unforgiving wilds
    Bruised, battered, undefeated

As the belly-fed chanting
Froze me with delight
I sank into the mystical moment
A simple wonder tendered it's beauty
Linking life to fleeting life.

She fled beyond my wanting grasp
And I alone with a stunned fountain of ink
As a distant hum mesmerized
The solitude of my day
    And still she sings.

The California Songbird

Expectantly, I cast my eyes
Towards the lofty rhapsody
As my feathered friend so merrily
Sings her song for me.

How sweet your morning serenade
That mingles with the breeze
Setting the stage-a-dancing
A million emerald leaves.

Branches wave in unison
Conducting your instrument
The anonymous concerto
A gift from heaven sent.

Majestic as the lulling flute
The sultry woodchimes sigh
And sinking towards your symphony
I gaze at the trembling sky

Secure within the ancient oak
You chant contentedly
And quietly I contemplate
How free your heart must be.

Perhaps I ne'er shall see
Your plumage red and gold

The peace within your sheltered soul
Shall remain to me untold.

Yet still I gaze in awe
At your theatre in the sky
With hope I'll glance your beauty
Before your wings shall fly.

Preface-The Flight Of The Bridalveil

Elizabeth and Feri bravely fled the confines of communist Hungary in 1957. On their wedding night they escaped across the frozen Danube. She was 84 years old when we first met in an Oregon vineyard. She shared her amazing story and seduced the words from me as the Cabernet descended.

The Flight of the Bridalveil

(For Feri & Elizabeth)

A swan skimmed over the Danube
The free world in her sight
As moonlight beamed a silver aisle
The honeymoon took flight

Beneath the wild Hungarian skies
He clutched the diamond-studded palm
Of his trembling bride.
Freedom lay on the other side
Frozen waters paved the way
As silently they stepped forth
Flapping unleashed wings
Scorning the chains of oppression.

Seasons of six decades galloped
She was 84 years young
When I, the lonesome wordsmith

15

Gazed into her dancing eyes.
She spoke of the sun's rising
And the skies bewildering beauty
The sipping of Chardonnay broadened her smile
Her joy was uncontained
Immeasurable as the fires in every life
She spoke of sausage making, bottling wine
And the craftiness of his loving hands.

No boundaries confine human dreams
Abandoning all fear
She fled into the grandeur of destiny
Having farewelled the Irish seas
I understand the significance of distance
And the tangled moments of separation.
A kindredness blossomed
As together we laughed
Beside St Josef's sleeping vines
Beneath the ominous clouds of Oregon skies.

Today the melted waters flow
As the river meanders gracefully
And reverberating within it's depths
The hushed embrace of whispered words
The eternal echoes of leaping hearts
The wedded ghosts of yesteryear
forever waltzing in unison

And still the flight of the bridal veil
And still the love of the bottled grape
And still the flapping of a bird released
And still her life…the great escape.

A Relic of
Dublin Town

And I a relic
Of the rare aul time
When a ten bob note
Made reason rhyme

Memories linger in my bones
The ever present shadows
Of yesteryear Dublin
A time of wondrous mingling
When a mere mouth utterance
Jingle Jangled the roar
Of laughter uncontained.

To-day all truth becomes a lie
The prowling tiger crawls
Through gaping streets of gold
Thieves kidnap my spirit
With their needle in the sky
And I in naked confusion
Swamped by the senseless rampage
As changing times pollute
The Liberties of my mind

No time for common decencies
No time for time itself
The daily human avalanche
Entrapped in a world wide web
Companioned by the bondage

Of a topped -up scavenger
So lonely and absurd.

Yet still with love delirious
I tread the cobbled veins
Of Dublin's world hidden backstreets.
Unleashed amongst the galloping heels
And child rampant lanes
I take refuge in the echoes
Of bygone ways and days
When all was grand
Within the penniless wealth
Of immeasurable simplicities.

My town, my own
They can't take you from me
With your pint-pouring Palace
Your ha'penny span 'tween north and south
And the elegance of a language
Proudly soaring through the mist
Of every human breath.

The pleasure is mine
To dwell amongst
The ghosts of ages past
And tolerate the Woodbined clouds
Of madmen flying
Towards life's complexities
And laughing rapturously
Until the open-armed
Canyons of death
Beg a kind repose from
The lovely wrath of it all.

And I a relic
Of the rare aul time
When a ten bob note
Made reason rhyme

In Praise of Guinness

The French are so proud of their Champs-Elysees
where madams so fragrant stroll by every day,

For the Brits it's nice tea served in china so fine,
and cricket on Sunday is simply divine.

The Welsh have their poets who sometime dig coal,
and fervently sing through their heart and soul.

The Scots have their Loch Ness with monster unseen,
and whiskey so smooth that it tastes like a dream.

The Yanks have their White House where freedom resides
with billions of dollars it expertly hides.

The Russians drink vodka to banish the cold,
while Lenin's fair dream still fails to unfold.

The Dutch have their red-lights and windmills so grand
in Spain they've their bullfights and miles of find sand.

Dear friends I concede that your treasures are grand
but there's one precious jewel that still leads the band.

In Dublin there's a beauty that just has no match
'Tis brewed near St. James' then thrown down the hatch.

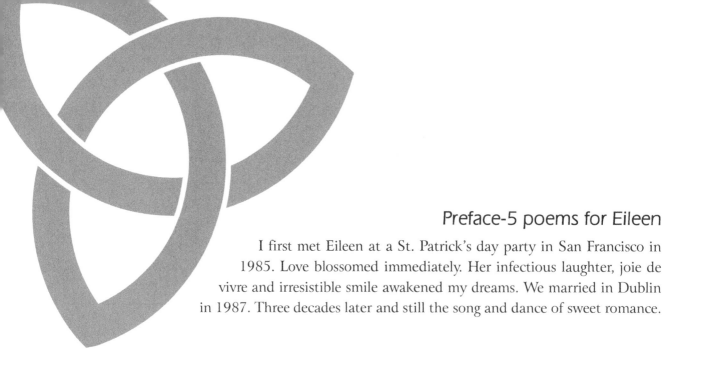

Preface-5 poems for Eileen

I first met Eileen at a St. Patrick's day party in San Francisco in 1985. Love blossomed immediately. Her infectious laughter, joie de vivre and irresistible smile awakened my dreams. We married in Dublin in 1987. Three decades later and still the song and dance of sweet romance.

WRAPPED IN RHAPSODY

(for Eileen)

She wandered
Into the harbour
Of my wildest woven dreams
Stumbling towards the blue
Of wide and mirthful eyes
A kind mysteriousness enflamed my world
A yearning from deep within
Stirred the passions of my heart
And in the quiet distance
The sun seeped through the sleeping clouds.

A flirt of life
A surging tenderness
A terrifying comfort
The birth of a new morning
The waters sang a sweeter tune
As we pranced along the enchanted way.

Two stars alight the midnight hour
Hungry hearts in a hungry space
A gentle breeze sways their course
The birth of love's enduring grace.

Our lives a windswept cabaret
Artist and wordsmith melting
Into the merciless arms of fate.
The colours of her riotous world
Blooming with the palette's anticipation
Mesmerized my senses
And I with trembling inkwell
Surrounded by whispering metaphors
Digging deeply for the waiting words.

An explosion of champagne
A thunderous laughter
A kitchen floor waltz
Soul mates wrapped in rhapsody
Dreamers drenched in reverie
Growing young 'neath the aging sun.

Two lovers gazing at the stars
The glimmering of moonlit beams
Her breath upon my sleeping face
The measure of a poet's dreams.

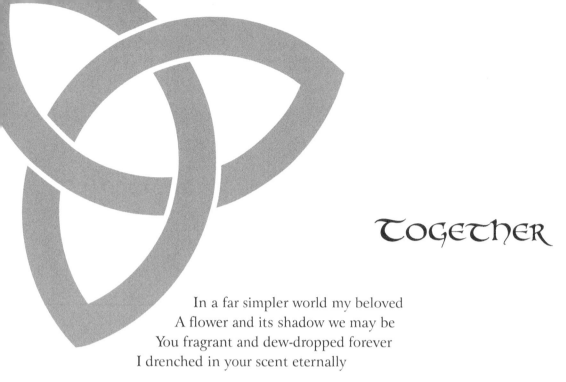

TOGETHER

In a far simpler world my beloved
A flower and its shadow we may be
You fragrant and dew-dropped forever
I drenched in your scent eternally

We'll dance with wild wind-tossed abandon
Beneath the cool shade of the trees
In rhythm with summer's soft whispers
In sway with the breath of the breeze

When sunlight enflames all your mysteries
And the artist goes wild with her art
I'll fade towards your burgundy petals
And tremble in the warmth of your heart

When the winds of our lives have subsided
And clouds shield the wintry sun
We'll drown in the arms of creation
And mingle forever as one.

A Snowflake
on My Mind

When I was wild with wandering
Unleashed like a mountain stream
An emptiness dwelled within
And love a distant dream

The sunrise offered tenderness
The seas a calm refrain
Yet my heart was rambling like a cloud
Through skies of seeping rain

My love was lonesome whisperings
I shared with frozen flowers
As silently they slumbered
Through the darkness of my hours

The moment touched me softly
Like a snowflake on my mind
Her smile enflamed a passion
Of a strange and wondrous kind

Now when seas and sunshine
Seduce a solemn trance
Beneath the golden rays I'll sing
On weaving foam I'II dance.

 23

WHEN LOVE CRAWLED IN

San Francisco '85
She threw me a champagne smile
Something wild from deep inside
Leapt towards the distant Heavens
I glanced at the Summer sky
Bright and blue
As the stardust in her eyes
Love crept slowly
I'd read the poems...enlightenment
I'd heard the tales...enchanting
My turn to drown in the scent of Oneness
A light shone through the darkness
We crawled into each other's lives
Waltzing beyond comprehension
In a world awash with mystery
A blessedness seeped forth
Joyous as butterfly wings
Sometimes I've cried like a storm
Emerging from a desperate calm
Sometimes I've laughed like a wind
Touched by the edge of Armageddon
Sometimes I've loved
Like nothing else exists
A creature soaked in rapture
Sometimes a wonder
Pours itself
As I imagine
Champagne raining from the starry skies.

As She Sleeps

Within our silent sanctuary
The whispered sighs subside
As dancing shadows fade
With the candles final foray

Horizoned in linen embrace
Cradled within the arms of Morpheus
You lie motionless
Linking yesterday's dream to the prayer of morn

As the piercing moonbeam
Penetrates the misty window pane
Upon your tranquil countenance
I softly lay breath upon breath reposed

My own eyes contentedly veil themselves
Child embraces weary child
As the scent of fragrant petals
Serenely sooths the pores of mind.

Preface-Mother [for Colette]

My mother was a French woman born in a small town called Mussy-Sur-Seine, 140 miles south east of Paris. My father a Limerick man met Colette on a beach near Avignon. I was born in Dublin in 1953..When I was nine months old my mother was diagnosed with schizophrenia . She returned to France and was placed in a hospital care facility where she lived for the remainder of her life. I was raised by my grandmother Mabel and my father Ted. They both died relatively young.

In 1984 with the assistance of marriage certificate details I located and visited my mother in l'Hospice Bar-Sur-Seine. I do not believe mere words are sufficient to describe the emotions. The spoken sentiments were softly whispered as the intertwining of hands and eyes filled the hours. Our love for each other was powerful. In five days we journeyed through three decades. The tears were reserved for the midnight silence. Colette passed away in 2001.

MOTHER

[for Colette]

Together at the birth
   of breathing life
Together at the fading
   of the light
And within the crawling years
Three wind-tossed decades
   of dreaming
About the warmth of an achingly familiar embrace.
In '53 the entirety of your world
Reflected in a lover's eyes

My father's eyes
    wide, rampant and blind
His sheltered vision gazed into the swamp
    of love's abyss
To see was to know too much
To know was to abandon love's demands.
A gentle touch
Steered your world to a place
Where angel's rest and weep
A gentle touch
And a restful womb
Cast breath upon wayward breath.

Your joy was momentary
    for soon, too soon
The waters divided life from blooming life
Your home became the confines
    of thoughtlessness
You remained forever young
Yet the spider webbed lines
Paraded themselves upon
    the face of time
Days were years and years eternity
And somewhere beyond the clouds
A galloping child
Engulfed by the precious wonder of his world.
No distance ever exists
    between mother and child
To think is to touch
To remember is to envision
To cry is to try
To understand
Yet an indescribable tenderness
Always embraces the hungry heart.
Before the end
I searched the green fields of France
I laid palm upon the tenderest palm
I laid eye upon the tenderest eye

And uncontrollably
Rested heart upon the tenderest heart.

You suggested a glass of wine
Had I a vineyard it was yours
The music of your words danced upon
    my trembling limbs
You spoke of yesteryears
When all was grand
Beneath your rainbow drenched skies
You spoke of howling winds
Far beyond your fragile grasp
We journeyed together
Through the perilous paths of
    times mysterious ways.
When the delicious Burgundy reached its end
We shared a smile
And listened to the deafening silence,
Another bottle filled the vacuum.
We waltzed from street to street
Along the love-soaked Seine
And nonchalant tree-lined ways.

Beyond the setting sun
Darkness advanced
Tears were reserved for
    the midnight silence.
I returned to Ireland
My ever present motherland
Three days later the skies clutched
    your final breath
Farewell the turning tides of time
Farewell the haunting unquenched fires
Tonight your tiredness rests
Within the sparkling stars
Tonight I stare at the distant sky
Tonight beneath folded eye
I too sleep
And dream the tenderest dream.

The Oul Fella

He let go
Laughing thunderously
As I Lindberghed my first two wheeler
The old Raleigh
Dynamo and all
Emptied his pocket
Yet filled his heart
As he eyed his child
Smothered in the purity
Of once off innocence.

Both bike and oul fella
Withered away
My wheels have since rolled
Through strong and gusty winds
Yet still his laughter echoes
As a time-trodden tenderness
Tickles the thoughts of mind.

Preface Soothing Tones [for Ger]

My cousin Geraldine is the matriarch of the family. She's the sister I've never had, the friend I've always had and the ever present guardian of my heartbeat

Soothing Tones

[for Ger]

I was in love with you
Before any understanding
Pierced my life
As a child I recall a glance
You flung my way
It hugged me reassuringly
I felt safe and equipped
To be thrown worldwide.
You always spoke softly
With words carefully chosen
From the canyons of books
And avenues of thought
That accompany your footsteps in time.
I just happened to be there
The lonesome recipient
Of your wisely ways
Sometimes oceans apart
Yet always touched by the fruitfulness

Of many soul-embracing moments
When life touched solitary life
As together we strolled
Towards Bewleys and beyond.
In the nakedness of a nearby hour
The beckoning waters
Will clutch me again
In their lovingly torturous way
As always the distance
Will unite us immeasurably
And beneath the same sky
We'll dance into the arms of destiny
I'll sail beyond your glance
And rest afar
Beneath the God-sent echoes
Of kindly whispered
Soothing tones.

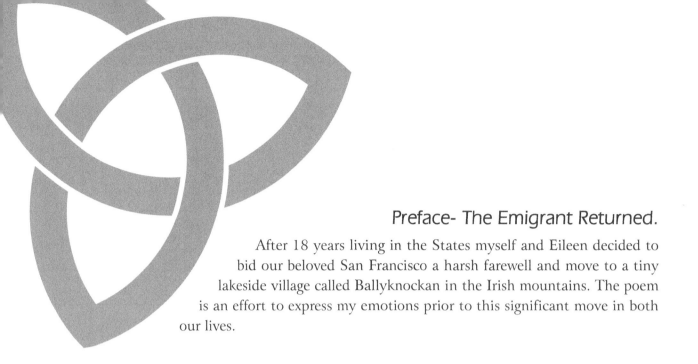

Preface- The Emigrant Returned.

After 18 years living in the States myself and Eileen decided to bid our beloved San Francisco a harsh farewell and move to a tiny lakeside village called Ballyknockan in the Irish mountains. The poem is an effort to express my emotions prior to this significant move in both our lives.

The Emigrant Returned

Swaggerin' beneath the Dublin skies
Trampling weather-beaten cobblestones
Nursery rhyming 'round rusty lamp-posts
Frenzied flight of youth and time
Dublin, mothering the motherless soul
Smothered between love and confusion
And I alone,
Glancing the fragility of it all.
So sudden, the wind blown flight of youthfulness
So intrusive, the whisperings of love's infancy
So beautiful, the warmth of a dirty old town,
So painful, the need to distance myself.
Farewell, womb-like embrace
Anna Livia's tempestuous temptings.
Farewell, youth's last lovely waltz
The boundless meanderings of innocence.
Suddenly quivering in the cradle of manhood
Muted to life's fearful mutterings

Clutched by the enticings of sun-kissed horizons
I fled it all.
Journeying aboard the spiraling sphere
Silently seduced towards a fog draped Golden Gate
Me, myself, I
In the flower-powered city of love
Agape, crawling, searching.
To vanished souls, unspoken words, were softly spoken
On vanished dreams, the wings of hope set sail
I listened to the water's ancient whisperings
I gazed as redwoods serenely shadowed the skies
I swam in the pools of human diversity
The indestructible spirit
Soared like a child's first breath.
As the dignity of truth and humility
Calmly touched the roots of consciousness
Endearingly, I reflected
Upon the pendulum's fleet-footedness
Life's blessings warmly reside in the pours of mind
The call to the wild viciously echoed itself
Peeping through the bridal-veiled mist
My eyes rested on pearls of blue
A tenderness touched my trembling heart
An angel embraced the wayward wanderer
Together we tread towards distant water's edge
And fled to the unyielding love of Dublin town.

Ballyknockan is a beautiful lakeside village nestled in the Wicklow mountains a mere 45 minutes from Dublin. Historically a home to granite stone masons, it's uniqueness was my home for eleven years, blessing me with friends, brothers in arms and God-sent serenity. Bidding farewell was a heart thumping step in my life.

PS. The lion and mother's child refer to the granite carved statues resting within the foothills of Silsean mountain on the edge of the village.

The Birth of Ballyknockan

She lay motionless
The mound of Silsean
Untouched by the hungry hands of time
Untrampled by frenzied flight
And deep within the silence
A sleeping lion unsculptured
A mother's child unborn
All alone
Within the drenched drowsiness
Of a lonely Wicklow hill.

Beneath the famined soil
In restful slumber
A diamond-eyed galaxy
Of jewels entombed in turf 'n time
The boulders of speckled granite
The silent observers of ages past

The unplundered heart of a sleeping colossus
All alone
Beneath the tearful skies
Of a lonely Wicklow hill.

All changed in eighteen and twenty four
The raging onslaught of hoof and heel
The hunger fed march of masons
Bewildered by the blinding trance
Of a mountain's wealth unveiled.
Within the grasp of clenched fist
The mighty sledge
Sinking deep into the weathered grain
Ravishing the eternal abyss
Of a lonely Wicklow hill.

A kind solemnness crept within
These anvil fisted quarrymen
The howling land begged them stay
Where the astral splattered sky
Reflected the nakedness of sparkling stone.
Seduced by the warmth of Summer's welcoming
They chose to lay limbs
Between the love-touched twinings
Of woven thatch
And the mingling of morning mist.

They lived within the warm embrace
Of stone upon carefully lain stone
From the land a sense of wonder
Whispering the ancestral echoes.
From the skies a scorching sun
Penetrating the pores of mind
And towards the midnight silence
A sigh of deep content soared
Into the lingering loveliness
Of a home called Ballyknockan.

ON LEAVING
BALLYKNOCKAN

A wild calling
An instinctive leap
From the clutch of stony walls
To the roar of distant seas
And the waiting womb of another world.

Farewell Silsean, Moanbane, Mullaghcleevaun,
Wicklow's clan of black-hilled warriors.
They'll find my foot prints, the God's of tomorrow
Cast in drenched muck and fiercely scented gorse
Molded with the warmth of a summer's breath.
I'll remain eternally with the ghosts of yesteryear
Hill-topped and wind swept beside the frostbitten cairn
Forever overlooking the village of sparkling stone.

Ballyknockan, you reached into the depths of my heart
Touching me with the pain of a deep kindness
Touching me with the warmth of a lover's grasp
Touching me with a decade of moonlit silence.
Your winds whispered to a listening life
Your sinking suns begged my tears to flow
Your waters waltzed with immeasurable calm
Your mountains forever offering refuge from the storm.

Solitary soul on Turlough Hill
Drifting clouds unveiling a newborn day

36

Red sika briefly danced and fled
Awakening my hour with joy uncontained.
Step after weary sodden step
Ascending the fog drenched hills
I searched for the mysteries of time
Hidden in the boggy flesh of a motherland
Sleeping 'neath the lonely lairs of antiquity
In passage tombs from megalithic moons.

Advancing along the ancient way
Through mist and rolling skies
Glendalough, the cradle of tranquillity
Grasps the rambling of my eye.
The monastic valley of two lakes
Chosen dwelling of a saintly soul
Illuminates the senses of my mind.
At the onslaught of the darkening hour
The sudden magic of a scorching sun
Stroking the canvas a shade of gold
All in a god-sent moment
Entwining the wonders of heaven and earth.

Ballyknockan, where strangers blossomed into friends
And friends forever brothers in arms
FAREWELL a word that steals my breath
Tossed by the winds and fragrant seas
My footprints were destined for further shores
One more night in the downhill-from-home tavern
And its life and limb on the western winds
Into the pulse of another day.

NO REST FOR THE POET'S EYE

No rest for the poet's eye
As a world of boundless mystery
Taunts the roving mind
Shadows crawling through burgundy skies
A lioness in the leaping seas
Hunger haunting a heavy heart
The staggering sight of time in flight
And the ever present inkwell
Braced in anticipation

No rest for the poet's ear
Chanting winds tickle the flight of imagination
Beyond eternity
Beyond horizons
Beyond today
Lies the whisper of God's reasonings
Meanwhile the scribe's companion
A metaphoric imagery
A rhyme of lonely syllable
And the birth of silent inspiration

No rest in the arms of slumber
Submerged in the nightly reprieve
Soaked in the astral freefall
Through the reverie of the darkened hour
A calmness stirs the beating heart

From the reservoir of poetic sound
A voice from far below
Mingles through the tangled web
And beside the quiet unconscious
The veer of quivering plume

No rest until the final descent
When deep amongst the sunken flowers
The spirit slowly releases
Journeying to the other side
And still a world of wild imaginings
Casts shadows and illusions
Towards the glance of poets
Drenched with life
Forever clutching the aspirant quill.

The Poet's Podium

The naked truth
And a roomful of listening
All eyes
All silent hungry eyes
Patiently perched
Upon the ragamuffin wordsmith.

Clenched within the poet's palm
The tortured pages of painstaking imaginings
Overflowing with swerve and crawl
Of inkwell dipped innuendoes.

The naked truth
Unveiled, tossed and hurled
Into the gaze of a gaping coliseum
All poems inextricably linked
The pen-pinched flaunts of life's parade
Tales of savage love
Twisted beyond the grasp
Of human reasoning.
Tales of fearless voyages
The whispered notions of tangled thought
The cluttered layers of veritable vagueness
And from the pinnacled podium
The breath of solitary life unleashed.

So why pretentious wordsmith?
Why?... the sharing of solemn secrecies

Where lies your penniless reward?
Perhaps amongst the hushed gathering
When the final word is flung
The kindness of a heart warmed glance
The gentle sigh of a touched soul
A gasp of understanding
The thrust of mind upon awakened mind
Such is the poet's gratification
As life's mysterious ways
Shivers into the pores
Of lonely souls-a-listening.

Dublin Aul Wan

Dublin aul wan, Sunday best, bag with spare few bob
Laughter in her glancing eyes, waltzing through the mob
Henry Street chocker-blocked, Moore Street bargain bound
Carrots, oranges, granny-smiths, ten for a green backed pound
Howaya luv, shockin' day, Evening or Heraldy Press
Wink of an eye, gentle sigh, off with the old "God Bless"
Kylemore bakery, cuppa cha, scone with jam and cream
Forty thousand calories, life's a bleedin' dream
Dunnes Stores, half-price, guaranteed Irish made
Frilly frocks, silky socks, daintily displayed
Dolphin Discs, Dickie Rock, show band memories
Grey-haired missis, reminisces, bygone pleasantries
Time for a tipple, Sandemans or perhaps a glass of white
Madigans or Slatterys, the afternoon delight
Shillings spent, heading home, time to cook him dinner
Yer man, herself, forty years, Dublin's saint and sinner
She watches children gallivant in their world that knows no fear
And pensively her deepest thoughts fly back to yesteryear
Journeying on the carousel of time's eternal dance
She still recalls the bittersweet taste of love's romance
Her world an unframed masterpiece, ambling through the breeze
Her life an unsung melody, rambling along the old quays.

DUBLIN

Dublin, a rare and gusty old town
Saturated in lunacy
Language, wild and explosive
Passion, alive as an inferno's flame
Howya head, fair play, poxy day, bang on
Echoes rippling like the Liffey's onslaught
Brazen knockers proudly plonked
On the brassed-up Georgian doors
And the udder knockers
Molly's marvellettes
Fondly fondled by the daily parade
Queen in a queenless town
Matriarch of mythology.
History spewing through our veins
And in the galloping blood
Gaiety of Viking venom
Fury of Celtic conquests
They came, they saw, we conquered
Then we stole their names, kept their castles
And embraced their madness.
The swagger of yer man
Saunterin' along the canal
Delira, excira, effin' and blindin'
Whistling through the raindrops
Eye-balling the swaddle of swanky swans
Irish Times quadrupled
Tucked tidily under the swinging elbow

Crossword completed.
Chislers beltin' balls
Jumpers for posts
Goalie gets it in the goolies
Back of the onion bag
One-Nil.
Brendan, James, Oscar, George
Anna Livia's literary legends
Feathered plumes ploughing
Through the myriad maze of cobblestones
Softly scribed syllables
Fables of Finnegan's bewildering wake
Jaysus Joyce!! Wha?
In the dip of an inky well
Their cadences captured a bygone time
When old triangles
Sufficed to symphonize
The heartbeat of a metropolis.
Ducks in the Green
Wagglin' under the lesser known O'Connell Bridge
U-turn at the bandstand
Then back to the splatter of a Buttercrust pan.
My own secret sanctuary
Under the sycamore's shade
Facing Emmet's postured poise
Water-edged with the whispering wrens
Biro in hand
Raking it all in
Grand.
Luke, Ronnie, Philo
First name basis
Blue blooded brothers
They scoffed the whiskey in the jar
Painted the dirty old town
Then fled into the annals of tomorrow's dawn
Statue stands beneath the tearful skies
Ace with the bass

Bronzed immortal.
And the weathered watering holes
A millennium of malicious gargling
The Long Hall, Mulligans, Palace Bar
Brazen Head, Willie Ryan's, Stag's Head
Proudly flaunting layers of history
Pint after patiently poured pint
Black stuff dark as the midnight sky
Full moon enticing upper lip
To silently sink into the depths of a foggy brew.
She fed me the stepping stones
The song and dance of a thousand years
I dove deeply into her grasp
My eyes opened wide
As the fires of awakening
Flung me into the howl of the human carousel
Always a seeping voice within
Always a permanence in my blood
Always Dublin.

In Full Flight

[for Tara]

Gone with the winds of yesterday
And to-day an eerie silence
Full flight, ears winged back, mouth agape
Her world a constant carnival.

So often she swam into my eyes
A warmth engulfing man and dog
Silently adoring
The preciousness of each other.

The mad anticipation
As bowed head dropped the retrievable twig
She's off , foaming saliva in full flight
Her tail the unleashed pendulum
As the limits of pure joy
Raged within the contents of a canine mind.

Her resting place
A world of shooting stars
And none safe from her grasp
I'll miss the gentle scratch of door
Footprints in the mucky gorse
The beat of thumping heart
Her ramblings from couch to bed
But most of all
Her coat as soft as angel's breath
As she fearlessly leapt
Into the welcome relief
Of my all embracing arms.

 46

Man's Best Friend

[for Toby]

He never shared his deepest thoughts
His secret ways I'll never know
His life the eternal pantomime
Footprints in the wintry snow.

Each hour a dawning masterpiece
Saliva dripping on his toes
Wide eyes agape with pondering
His bark the unpenned canine prose.

We danced together through the years
Laughter dragged us to our knees
Through winds and waves and frosted peaks
We fled from life's realities

He'd often stare relentlessly
Into the canyons of my eyes
A stroke, a kiss, a tenderness
So often caught me by surprise.

His final hour came suddenly
He vanished swiftly around the bend
My sadness danced with memories
Of wagging tails and man's best friend..

47

Thoughts on the Human Spirit

A low and weakened man
In the hour of uncertainty
Beneath the dreary darkness
A cruel trembling thrusts
It's venomous fury
Upon a blind confusion.

In silent desperation
In the still of shrouded somberness
An emptiness crawls within
A crumbling loneliness
Weighs upon the reasonings
Of low and weakened man.

Above the fear, a pulsating power
Prowling through blood and bone
The silent sentinel
The sleepless vigilante
The arousal of an untamable force
Defiant as the onslaught of time.

The rising of a wounded warrior
Companioned by a raging spirit
The resurgence of a dignity
Dreaming the distant dreams

Clawing from the depths of resistance
The fearless fiber of understanding.

Into his world a love retrieved
A whispering from the birth of time
His warming eyes agape with passion plundered
From a light between the prayer of morn
And the slumbering of a moonlit trance
......and still a towering powerfulness.

Alive at last, man's awakening
Bewildered by life's boundless excess
The uncaged bird in hungry flight
Surrendering to the waltzing of winds
Dancing to the rhythm of a pounding pulse
Alive, within a world of timeless wonders.

The Itchy Feet Syndrome
(TRAVELLER'S DILEMMA)

Steered by the lure of trampling seas
Wild as a meandering star
I flew upon the vagrant winds
An somewhere within the vast abyss
Lay the awaiting shoreline of my life

Caught in a whirlwind
Too powerful the tempting of unseen horizons
Such is the traveller's dilemma
Such circumstance paved the emigrant's way
Journeys carved in dirt and sea and wanderly sky
Each a temporary retreat
Each finely tuned
To the thumping wind song of a wondrous world.

Seasons reeled into years
And I a frantic dreamer
Crawling through the layers of time
Home appeared unexpectedly
I stumbled into my secret sanctum
Where winds and waters chimed
And silence offered contemplation
Beneath the haunting Irish skies

Farewell the scampering of a searching soul
Today a sacred peacefulness
Today a life at ease
All calm, terribly calm
Until the masts of tomorrow's breeze
Seduce the waves of a beating heart.

MOTHER NATURE'S SON

And in the garden
Far from the shadows of man
She stole me away
Begging me to abandon all time
And lose myself
In her world of scented seedlings
The mother of morning's mysteries
And the son of a wavering world
Together in lovingly soaked pourings
Between heaven's blue domain
And the infinite clay beneath.

A welcome sigh filtered
Through the veins of my thoughts
Upon the dancing green grasses
And the sway of falling petals
I rested momentarily.
An indescribable kindness
Accompanied my great escape
Into the unsinkable bliss
Of a wind-kissed sanctuary.

Lost in a maze of mindlessness
Through gaping flower and blossomings
A mountain ash caught my eye
It's outstretched limbs
Conducting the endless waltz
Of leaping leaves and love-touched things.

 52

I bowed lowly and captured
The fragrance of a maternal breath unleashed
Into the pastures of time and space.

Beneath the warmth of Burgundy sky
Engulfed by the buzzing of abounding life
I then embraced the solitary self
At home in the verdant palm
Of a whispering haven,
And I, mother nature's son
Although in lingering solitude
Whilst drenched in mist and mystery
No loneliness can touch my beating heart.

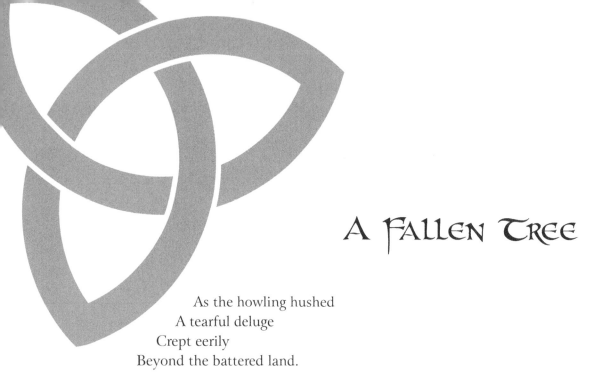

A Fallen Tree

As the howling hushed
A tearful deluge
Crept eerily
Beyond the battered land.

A welcome luminescence
Filled the ebony sky
A somber silence ambled
As the morning's rising
Unveiled the wrath of time.

She lay motionless
Helplessly horizoned
In the open-tombed wilderness
Still garbed in emerald splendour
As weeping sap sighed and spilled
Over your sleeping steeple.

Upon your limbs no robins rest
No breeze shall flaunt within your grasp
Nor sun alight your leafy limbs
Farewell my weathered warrior
Still draped with poise and dignity
Slowly seeping, sinking, crumbling
Towards the worm-filled warmth
Of the womb-a-waiting.

Preface- Poet Of The Land

Patrick Kavanagh born in Inniskeen, County Monaghan is arguably Ireland's greatest poet since W.B. YATES. A complex genius, more comfortable in rural farmland surroundings than the glossy lights of Dublin. Worthy recognition eluded him during his lifetime. His essence was Irishness personified.

POET OF THE LAND

(FOR PATRICK KAVANAGH)

Hidden beneath the mossy soddened turf
Lay the unembroidered roots of your heart
Your dreams stretched
Towards the wisdom of Anna Livia
Yet the fields of Monaghan
Echoed every creaking branch
And sprouting seed
Whispering your secrets.
They begged your return
To seek a second childhood
Amidst the violets, your only daughters
And the fields that called you son.

A falling leaf soaked with the dew of morn
Rested in your palm
Such a fine quill, you smiled
And inked it's moisture on a sodden bark

55

You alone touched the soul of the quiet man
And ploughed deep towards the birth
Of his unuttered words.
There lay a land
Where clay and roses shared respect

Alive at last, you wrote of joys
That ne'er crossed the threshold of kings
The love of a thorny briar
Blanketing a bed of moss
A nameless windswept road
Leading to the finger touching tip o' the cap
A quiet pint where eyes connect and bless the moment
With a whisper of the native tongue
Still clinging to it's deathbed
The saliva dripping glance of a faithful friend
Ever panting with anticipation
The glowing scented turf
As it warms the aching flesh
At last, at last unbent
Upright with knee clutching dignity.

When the skies beckoned
The stony hills of Inniskeen
Draped your smile with clay
Your soul mingled with the worms
The winds granted a moment's silence
Fallen petals gathered themselves
And laid your only wreath.
As poet of the land
Your fortune lay ungathered and unsought
By the slums of mind,
Yet forever clung to the coins of simplicity
Perhaps contentment's deepest seed.

The Cuppa Tea

Before the awakening
Of sleep wrenched mind
The lip-sipped infusion
Before plunging
Into morning's grasp
The brim filled cup of warmth
Before conversation with self
And those in the maddening crowd
The piping hot caffeine pot.

The ancient ritual
Finger plucked
From distant Darjeeling
And Ceylon's fertile slopes
The fragrance filled
Rusty green leaves
Lovingly sun scorched
Crumbled and seabound
Towards the four corners
Of a world seduced.

Dancing kettleful
Whistling lifesong
Pouting sssssteam
Silver spoonful
The self indulgent
Anticipation
Time for the aromatic
Pampering
Of a soothing sup
….China cupped pick me up.

The Hummingbird's Farewell

Two years within each others worlds
Sharing life's little weavings
She hummed and fluttered joyously
Savouring the sugary banquets
Her gravity defying feats
A wonder to my glancing eye
In weathers warm, cruel and mild
Her flapping wings forever wild.
The sight stalled my breath
Just beyond the welcome mat
So terribly motionless and curled
She lay wrapped in a lifeless poise
Kneebent and playful I begged
For the beat of a breathing breast
I slowly fingered her folded wings
Her parting gesture clawed my guts
A miraculous flash of feathered crimson
Her eyes remained deadly curtained
Weightless in my trembling palm.
Beside the spring-draped dogwood
It's leaves also crimson blushed
Dancing with the westward winds
I scooped a mere handful of clay

Her teacup sized resting place
Watered my wavering eye
Down into the waiting womb
A shadow, two majestic inches
Lowered into an eerie peacefulness
Restful yet forever humming
Through the depths of my sunken consciousness.

The 50A Bus

Upstairs was best
As she rolled and rollicked
Over weather-beaten cobblestones
The dirty green double-decker
Chariot of Raglan Road
Limousine of Dublin town
Puffing and pouting
Through Coombe and Viking built womb
Last stop Nelson's head
Long gone 'nuff said.

Upstairs was best
Conversation rampant as a hungry worm
Best between aul wans
Complaining about the slithery stink of life.
Visibility stolen
By lairs of Woodbine smoke
The mingle of morning fog
And gossipy gargled breath
One swipe of the duffler's elbow
Window pane demystified
And the show begins

Front row seat grand and royal views
All the way for less than a bob
Delicious earful of bollocking banter
Co-cough-any of throatful pourings
Allegations flung from ear to waxy ear

Rustle of Indo and Heraldy Press
Strangers sitting arse to maggoty arse
Conductor on a roll
Fares please, poxy day
Thanks a million and he's off
To the next victim.

Conductor swaggers through the gauntlet
Next stop Dolphin's Barn
There's a bleedin' name for ya
Neither farm nor maritime creature in sight
'Scuse me I'm getting off
Knees to the right
Arse rubs weary face
Great value for a tanner.
Inspector on board
The uncrowned prince of Ringsend
Fancy hat and attitude
Time to unravel ticket
From left index finger
There ya are boss
Dirty glance no thanks.

Clery's in sight, I'm off
Thumb to red button
Driver thanked with mumbled sincerity
His response a barbaric grunt
His final gesture
Mouthful of fuming exhaust
Faceful of flying puddle
Screech of Kilkenny remould

Free at last
As the 50A fades
Into the familiar renown
Of me darlin' jewel
Dublin town.

Dublin 2013

I watched you crawl
When the 50's were on their knees
Punters scrambling to stitch it all together
Children darting like meteorites
Stuck in the warmth of a rare old time
Our wealth lay in the sea of kindness
That drenched every bleeding heart
And nourished the cradle of our dreams.
Beneath the drizzle of grey skies
A stampede of blazing lives
Each soul soaked in a language
Poetic as the breath of young life

She arose, my dirty old town
Into the shiny heights of a new dawn
Gone are the whips of skipping ropes
The songs of youthful animosity
The frugal stretching of a ten bob note
And the neighbourly quips of brothers-in-arms.
Yet still the Liffey waters run
Beside the footprints of yesterday's world
Entombed in the ripples of her mossy depths
The resounding laughter of a bygone day
When wit was launched by the glint of an eye
And every word a timely splattered masterpiece

Something died from deep inside
As the greed of a roaring tiger

Prowled through the veins of a hungry town
Dublin, adorned in unaccustomed splendor
Loftily sailing aboard the sinking ship
Stepped aside, from the ways of a thousand years.
"As she wheeled her wheelbarrow
Through streets broad and narrow."
Still the soothing avalanche of song
Poet's gazing at the howling rains
Laughter meandering through the foggy dew
And lover's drenched in mystery
As Anna Livia's matriarchal glance
Seeps through wide and brazen eyes.
Into the furnace of our beating hearts.

INSPIRATIONS

Stolen
From the canyons of consciousness
As the poet's musings mingle
A fanciful thought
Churns the embroidered word.

Shadows flung from dancing petals
Tease the roving mind
The birth of morning's mysteries
Clutch the sleepy eye
The sky and thoughts of distant fields
The sea and hidden fin-flapped ramblings
The forest shouldered by tranquility
Seasons circled in timeless hibernation

Fables, folklore, faery myths
Flowers, friendships, frozen dreams
Tempestuous ragings howling
And music, the piper's elbow
Softly seducing the mystical air
The fiddler's fingers fondling
Wrinkled grains of pampered oak
The spirit rising above the pain
That twists the thorn within
Children delightfully entranced
With days of dance and lullaby
And love, the eternal chain's unbroken link
The powerful purpose of it all.

Such fleeting joys and sorrows
Awaken my restless slumbering
All these kind inklings
Weave the inky birth of light
Plucking the strings of inspiration
As feathery quill ambles
Upon gaping vacant line
And I a lonesome wordsmith
Adrift with folded eye
In silence searching
For the final tangled fusion
Of passion's heartfelt metaphor
Scrolled in rhyme and time.

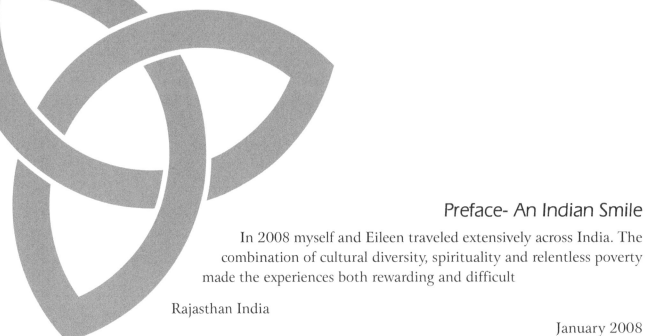

Preface- An Indian Smile

In 2008 myself and Eileen traveled extensively across India. The combination of cultural diversity, spirituality and relentless poverty made the experiences both rewarding and difficult

Rajasthan India

January 2008

AN INDIAN SMILE

India
A waterfall of humanity
Each drop plunging frantically
Beneath the vast and quivering sky

Drenched in colour
Sapphire, gold, burgundy, magenta
A rainbow of silken opulence
Adorning the parade of perennial poverty

Long departed, the all conquering Mughals
And uninvited colonialists
Their palatial grandeur and sandstone forts
Remain…filling the eye with awe

Backdropped by the Rajasthani fortress
The Jaisalmer spice lady
Lowly crouched, still as morning light
Surrounded by the aromatic delights

Nourished from the trembling heart
Of a trembling India

Her dark eye grasped the wandering of my own
Her face intricately graced by the ways of time
Her hunger visible as the beauty in her soul
I know so little of her worries
Her burdens and mine bear different weights
Her eyes speak in silent communication
I know so little of her loves
Yet love abounds in every beating heart
It comforts the sadly disturbed
And disturbs those wrapped in comfort

Eye to hungry eye
And I drown in the warmth of her glance

Our minds softly intertwine
Her smile is cast unexpectedly
Not a broad faced outburst
Just a gentle hint
A brief emotional escape
Sparse
As the wink of a sparrow's eye

My own smile released itself
Our lives danced together for an eternal instant
Her years had crawled beyond
The sorrowful searching for charity
No outstretched rupee-seeking palm
Just a hunger waiting to be fed

She warmed me more than the midday sun
I chose a handful of green and orange
She whispered rupees two and four
Her voice both tranquil and intoxicating
I placed the coins within her grasp

Her smile returned, this time accompanied
By a new found breath of life
Something inside of me wept for joy
In the India I have briefly known
Kindness is immeasurable
And love as common as every grain of sand

Yet keep within lie mysteries
Unveiled to the searching eye

As evening beckoned
Silence soaked the sleepy night
The full moon rose towards the distant skies
Streets were hushed and slumbering

I lay in the arms of wonder
The wonder of a magical land
The wonder of a billion souls
And deep within my restlessness
…the wonder of a lonely smile.

Preface-The Weeping Bull [for John Hayes]

During England's long occupation of Ireland speaking our native Gaelic language or playing our national sports of Gaelic football and hurling was forbidden. In defiance the Irish marched onto Dublin's Croke Park in 1920 and proceeded to play football. The English [Black and Tans] response was to open fire shooting 14 civilians dead. 87 years elapsed. Then in 2007 the English rugby team ran onto Croke Park's revered grass [for the first time since] to face the boys in green. During Ireland's national anthem the Irish prop forward John [the Bull] Hayes was seen visibly shaken and shedding tears. Such passion should have been a warning to "the old enemy" for what lay ahead. I watched the game in Songhkla, a Muslim town in southern Thailand. Final score; IRELAND 43 ENGLAND13

The Weeping Bull

They sang their song
The rose scented charioteers
Then we sang ours
And brought a raging bull to tears

Upon the blood stained grass
The Munster man with head held high
As thoughts of 1920
Filtered through his watery eye

He voiced the ancient soldier's song
With fists clenched by his side

His mighty frame was trembling
And drenched in emerald pride

Another page in the history book
Today old wounds are healed
With years of faded memories
Unleashed on a Dublin field

Silence and restrained respect
For the enemy in white
But soon her majesty would know
What it's like to lose a fight

No more weeping from the bull
He's answered the plight of Ireland's call
With his heart the size of Connaught
And his hunger for the oval ball

I'll never forget the mighty man
Shaking beneath the Dublin skies
His gaze grasped by the heavens
Where the green flag proudly flies

He touched the pulse of a nation
And reminded us with ease
That the enemy were only great
When we were on our knees

Today we rose with dignity
And flew like a bird released
With Croker soaked in passion
And the tears of a gentle beast.

IRELAND 43
ENGLAND 13

The Hawaiian Garden

Upon your emerald tapestry
So verdant and serene
The forest swayed enticingly
Towards the sun's half hidden gleam.

The banyan's mighty outstretched arms
Embraced my weary mind
As life's incessant momentum
Released it's constant bind.

I glanced in contemplation
At this garden by the sea
Where nature shared and nurtured
In peace and harmony.

From Seychelles Isles and Mozambique
The flora traversed the foam
To blossom in distant sanctuary
Their Polynesian home.

Reflected in the lily lake
Your heart reposed with calm
As rippling fragrance whispered
Beneath the swooning palm.

Beside the Onomea falls
I begged my soul to rest

And mingle 'midst the wonder
Of a mother's fertile breast.

The remembrance of your grandeur
Has set my spirit free
And should my life touch sorrow
I'll cast a thought towards thee.

Preface Farewell [for Jessie]

Jessie was a homeless Vietnam veteran whose short life ended on the streets of San Francisco. His humour and kindness of spirit enriched my day whenever we spoke.

FAREWELL

[for Jessie]

Motionless
As death's companion
You whispered dime, nickle, penny
Crouched amongst feathered scavengers
Upon pavements cracked and cold
Home from long lost motherless home
Your suffering silently crawled
Towards the darkened moment of release.
Wrinkled mirrors of your soul
Exposed the terrifying roar
From distant fields of destruction
Long since reposed in silence
Yet incessantly echoing
Within the canyons of mind.
As scent of cappuccino lingered
Teasing battered senses
Lowly, you whispered with outstretched palm.
Faces fresh from feathered slumber

Paraded around your depravity
Farewell depravity
Farewell the pain of insignificance
Farewell the faint remembrance of tenderness.
As wine stained vagabond caressed the fading light
Your heart paused beneath the flickering blanket
And silently fled to silver lined clouds
Where the warmth of dignity
And life anew embraced
The gentle whisper of a soul untouched.

Preface So Alone [for Terri]

Terri was my next door neighbour in San Francisco. We shared a small back porch where she loved to listen to the music of Van Morrison and Johannes Brahms. She sadly took her own life on Moss beach. The music was silenced forever.

So Alone

[for Terri]

Alone, so alone
You quenched out the light
A new star shines brightly
In the dark distant night.

And as you repose
With the angels above
I pray that you bloom
Like a flower blessed with love.

Farewell to the flame
That burned deep inside
The fire that Brahms
Had failed to subside.

A constant companion
So tortured your heart

Then from this fine world
You choose to depart.

The violins sighed gently
As friends bid adieu
To a fragile young life
That only God knew.

Like the rose of last winter
So cold and unseen
Your summer awaits
In the sky so serene

Preface-The Man They Called Garcia

Jerry Garcia was the leading member of the legendary San Francisco band The Grateful Dead. Their iconic status and cult following still "weeds" it's way through the flower powered city of love. Garcia died in 1995.

The Man They Called Garcia

The stars are shining brightly on the astral stage so dark
Far from the mother planet where their music left it's mark
Hendrix sits upon a cloud and masters every chord
The maestro lives unequaled jamming with the Lord
He dreamed of a companion whose lyrics gently sigh
Imagine how he smiled when Lennon passed him by
John, "please stay and rest a while," he whispered through the air
Together on that dove white cloud they lived without a care
Soon within the mighty sky a drummer did appear
As Keith banged on that floating moon they shed a joyous tear
"We need a voice" said John, like thunder in the night
So Janice sat upon that cloud and roared with all her might
Embracing one another they praised serenity
And silently recalled a world that lacked simplicity.
For those remaining on the path between what's right and wrong
They linked their minds together and wrote a simple song
"To play this song for those below," said Janice with a smile
We need a guiding guru to rest for just a while
Then suddenly a shooting star landed by their side
And the man they called Garcia proved he never died.

The Troubadour of Gin-Joint Sleaze

(For Tom Waits)

Voice like rolling rubble, fueled by bourbon's imagery,
Mind like drunken windmill, swirling wild and carelessly
Fishnet tights, bar stool nights, prelude to the welcome bed
Vowels 'n growl's n' metaphors, smoke rings in a fiery head.

Troubadour of gin-joint sleaze, poet of closing-time thinking
Notions with wings, strummer of strings, piano that's always been drinking,
His best friends are brawlers, midnight crawlers, unleashed in the misty charade,
Their eternal cocoon, the last chance saloon, stuck in the beer stained parade.

Angelic as a satanic relic, religion's not his heart's desire
God in a bottle makes Tom's throat throttle, as croaking notes soar higher
His hobbies are hookers, dubious good lookers, clinging to the last drop of wine
Small change boozers, dead end losers, searching for a blue Valentine.

Lover of the obscure, the slightly impure, the tasty whore from the perfumed sewer
Lover of bars, Cadillac cars, Venus and Mars, Havana cigars
Frequenter of slums with down-trodden bums, drenched in the scent of Ja-maican rums
Waitsman on a rampage, Waitsman on a roll, touching my senses, touching my soul

He writes of life's complexities red eyes stumbling down a cul-de-sac
Trembling hearts with passions pledged, mule variations on a one way track

In a world of vague obscurities I listen to the deafening roar
Of a voice entwined with poetry that pierces to the core.

    Waits I'll never know your mind
    You'll always leave me guessing
    Yet swimming through your tortured vowels
    Has been a painful blessing.

LIFE BEGINS

[@ 40]

When I have sauntered on a dream
To frosted peaks that pierce the skies
And lingered restful by a stream
Whose beauty haunts and mystifies.

When I have cried a million tears
And seen blue pearls through bridal veil
It's then I'll cease to count the years
And seek the breeze to fill my sail.

When I have laughed at life itself
And smiled into a stranger's eye
And reread poems upon the shelf
That make my heart both smile and sigh.

When I have buried seeds of hate
Then learned to love life's trepid ways
And welcomed through my garden gate
All signs of hope to share my days.

'Tis then the wrinkles may appear
And weave and roam and intertwine
I'll treasure tales of yesteryear
And boast I'm one past thirty-nine.

Barely Alive

Nine to five barely alive
Howling winds unfold
Hungry eyes are crawling
Through wretched streets of gold.

Entangled in a frenzied haze
Ravished world in flight
Clutched within a whirlwind
From morn till hush of night.

All the rush-fooled warriors
Journeys twisted blind
Entrapped amongst the senseless
Throngs of hurried mind.

Tormented souls like shadows chased
Beyond the grasp of time
Beyond the soothing silence
Where woodlands softly chime.

Before the veil of life descends
And judgment hour is nigh
Rest beneath the whispering leaves
Throw glances at the sky.

In a world of blind confusion
Where children scarcely dance
Tread gently through the weaving winds
And hear your heartbeat dance.

"HITTING 60"

I laid my sight upon a galloping child
Crazed in unbridled glory
Fueled by the wonders of his world
Echoes of laughter resounding
Amidst the mysteries of a perfect life

The dance of yesteryear resurrected itself
Dublin in the rare old times
The back lane my coliseum of valour
Chasing bees 'neath apple trees
And all ya need is love, love, love.

The winds have tossed me kindly
when mountains stood in my way
I sneered the wrath of adversity
Scaling the misty heights
Into a whirlwind of guiding light.

Gracefully, she walked into my eyes
And set my heart ablaze
We swayed into each other's worlds
And a million midnight moons later
The song and dance of sweet romance.

An unwelcomed visitor strolled into my life
The one that follows fifty-nine
I balanced myself upon the flight of time

Allowed the escape of a frugal smile
And vowed to stay forever young.

I laid my sight upon a galloping child
His hopes still in their infancy
A solemnness swept over me
As softly I stepped forward
Into the grasp of tomorrow's dreams.

TIME

(Thoughts on Ageing)

Time to reverse time itself
Time for life's unchained refrain
Time to shine like the morning sun
Time to elope with the world again

Time for poetics of wind song
Time to plough the whispering vowel
Time to verse the epilog
Time for Heaven's awakening howl

Time to ride the wildest waves
Time to shed a joyous tear
Time to grasp elusive dreams
Time for the child to reappear

Time to quench life's raging thirst
Time to pluck the ripened vine
Time to taste forbidden fruit
Time to savour vintage wine

Time for glancing at the moon
Time to dance 'neath weeping skies
Time for love's next episode
Time to drown into her eyes

Time to master the mandolin
Time to script life's soulful song
Time to unveil mysteries
Time to prove the whole world wrong.

PRAYER

And with the encroaching darkness
The final words of the forsaken
A knee bent whisper towards the fading light
A begging for understanding
A desperate plea for the Maker's mercy

The silent murmur of a shackled soul
Escaping the brutality of loneliness
Floodwaters rising around his world
God his only audience
And prayer a lifeline to the skies

In the bloodstained fields of history
In the fear of an outstretched palm
In the seeking of forgiveness
In the time of heaven's calling
As the bells are sounding from-a-high

When a soulmate softly slips away
A life is drenched in solitude
There's healing in the Father's words
And in the quiet of the night
Spirits swoon towards the guiding light

In a world that's cloaked in mystery
There's hope in the dreamer's dreams
There's power in the hungry heart
Then when the judgment hour is nigh
The final word, the final sigh.......

A Swerve of Life

(Dublin to Portland)

Oregon,
Today the wonders of your wilds
Quenching my deepest desires
Beneath the allure of cascading falls
Inhaling the bounty of verdant slopes
Lustfully indulging myself
In the rouge of Cabernet vines
With the trembling ticking of life's pendulum
Time to grasp the feintest star
Abandon the breath of all reason
And within the thunder of your mighty waters
Roar together until the beckoning hour

Today the land where dreamers dwell
Plodding the pioneer paved ways
Beneath the tapestries of fallen leaves
May your forests steal the echoes
Of my softly sown prayers
Sometimes a howling from beyond
Whisperings from the Liffey swell
Longings from the deepest core
In such darkened hours
I'll cling to freshly laid roots
Leap with laughter unleashed
And dance insanely
When a human touch
Wraps itself around the contours of my life

Having flown like a migrating bird
I landed upon a million sparkling lights
Each a flickering soul
Floating aboard the human ark.
Revellers of the great Northwest
And a son of the Celtic diaspora
All travelers in the wilderness
Let's crawl together into each other's hearts
Free as the ocean's wrath
Wild as the wild Columbia
And bathe in the depths of emerging love.

In Manzanita I closed my eyes
And surrendered to a silent awakening
A voice from beyond.
The heavens cried as the ocean's final leap
Drenched the shoreline of my heart
The waters aired a familiar refrain
A tenderness arose from deep within
A swerve of life
Warm as the fires of a distant land.
Before the sinking of the sun
A sighful breath released itself
I gazed into the raging seas
And kissed the embers of the sky.

REFLECTIONS OF IRELAND

She appears
In the ominous windgusts
Of Oregon's western skies
Clouds crawling lustfully
Lunging beyond the fading light.
Further east lies Dublin
The town that coaxed my awakening
Then gently let me fly.
I packed her with me
In the parceled memories
Of urchins mesmerized by the mysteries
Of life's emerging flames

And in the untampered beauty
Of Manzanita's misty miles
As cliffs and waters collide
Mirroring the majesty
Of Ireland's seaswept slopes
Where puffins plunge precariously
As the winds sing in unison
And the fabled faeries frolic
With whispers from the ancient land.

In the eyes of the pioneer dreamers
Passions packed and Columbia bound
Planting their newfound lives
Where rivers leap and haunt
Within the depths of migrating minds.

88

1845 eyes west
Fueled by the breath of despair
The flight of a hungry nation
Famished sons of Erin
Their songs well versed
Tuned to the sighs of the saddening seas

Atlantic northwest
Pacific northwest
I bow beneath your common sky
To-day the streets of Portland town
Trampling leaves of gold and brown
As the sparrow softly sings
I hear the distant mandolins.
My home lies where the skylark soars
Wild is the call of the untamed breeze
And somewhere in the distant shores
The lure of freedom's fragrant seas.

The Front Porch

Shelter from the multitudes
Den of illicit pleasures
Tavern, library, office,
Coffee shop, V.I.P. Lounge, planetarium,
Thumb and index finger
PSSSCHH!! Happy Hour
Alaskan Amber ale
Slowly poured into tilted stein
Rising foam adding dignity
To the corner store 6-pack
I grab the travel section
Lose myself in the turquoise waves
Of another world
Martinique, book today, 25% off
Complimentary prosecco upon arrival
Fools rush in.
PSSSCHH!!
My haven is 10x4
Benny is 1 foot 1 inch
His tail veers towards the sunny side.
He ignores the birds
Grunts at the cats
Tolerates the squirrels
Hates the bees
Fears the sirens
And loves me beyond description
Harmony of growl and bark

He critiques my poetry
All wagging tail approvals
He's the shadow on my shadow
The stabilizer of my weathered ways
The porch his canine sanctuary
PSSSCHH!!
Humming birds, here, gone, flash of red
Sparrows and redbreasts
Combat for scattered crumbs
Fiesty little survivors
They dump the unwanted seeds
Crap on my Welcome mat
I love them
Flowers face sunward
Maples blush into autumn
Neighbour saunters by
Howdy, PSSSCHH!! PSSSCHH!!
We discuss Tom Waits,lucky ladies and microbrews
The synchronicity of hungry hearts
Mingling of muse and mirth
Our world a momentary masterpiece
Aligned in beerful harmony
He's off, night Nate, solitude
Another neighbour
No smile, no wave
His paltry poodle looks bored.
Sinking sun bids adieu
Flaunt of a familiar shadow
She pours a vodka, dash of cranberry
Plonks posterior into wicker
Wife of almost three decades
The blissful beneficiary of my ways
Evening breeze is warm and hushed
We sink into each other's worlds
Benny gets a kiss, a hug, a squish, and a "there's a good boy"
I get one of the above
Sun fades, stars flicker, moon beams

Crickets chant their nightly drone
Little windows illuminate
Peace abounds
Benny's eyes fold
I grab her hand
Count the stars
And feel the weight fly away
PSSSCHH!!
ZZZZZZZ.....

ḢOMELESSNESS

As the chill of darkness
Cruelly penetrates the bones of breathing life
Do dreams offer solace
From the wrath of hunger's relentless growl

Morning creeps through the alleyway
The city's heartbeat thumps
To the swarm of encroaching life
There's a welcoming warmth
In the burst of morning sun
And beneath the frozen blanket
A murmur of trembling humanity
As a lonesome soul unfolds
Into his world of hope and desperation

An emptiness lies
In the plea of an outstretched palm
A sadness aches
In the lifeline of a faltering dignity.
Have your prayers gone unheeded
Are divine powers beyond your grasp
Or has your Godly saviour
Chosen the hour of redemption
When love may rain unselfishly
As the heavens pave the sacred way.

He stands motionless
As the stampede of manicured life

Cast their saddened glances
And from the kindness of man
Pennies drop
Crumbs of human compassion
Birdsong fills the midday sky
Creatures sing, creatures fly.

The heat of daylight slowly fades
Ravens seek their sheltered nest
A shadow drenched in loneliness
Lays down his sunken limbs to rest.

HOW TO WRITE A POEM

A voice
Must be found
Within the whirlwind of silence
Then carved into rhyme and reason

An imagination
Must fly beyond
The boundaries of creation
Then sail upon the breath of young life

Language
Must rise from the reservoirs
Defying the confines of vision
Then mingle, muse and mystify

Passion
Must dance wildly
Like the fires of the universe
Flaming towards the crest of enlightenment

A mind
Must be transported
To a place within the mystic
Then pray for Divine intervention.

Awakening

Soaked in contentment
Burdens cast aside
The freshness of morning air
Enticing me to drown
In the wonder of a tender quietness.
The awakening sun peeps
Over mistful hills
With a stroke of quivering gold
Waters illuminate
I lustfully inhale
Life's fragrant offerings
Peace abounds
Yet still a silent desperation
A sadness swaying within
As I plunge solemnly
Into the simplicity
Of how things ought to be.

The Man Above

In the mystical flight of the hummingbird
In the throbbing of its wings
In the crumbling leaves of autumn time
In the joy of mysterious things

In the gasping breath of an infant child
In the leap of a pounding heart
In the folding eye of a fading life
In the spirit bound to depart

In the beauty of life overflowing
In the warmth of a lover's tear
In the blindness of misunderstanding
In the trembling of hatred and fear

In the weaving of a spider's web
In the curve of a mountain stream
In the poet's inspiration
In the silence of a midnight dream

At one with the skies and heavenly stars
At one beneath the deepest seas
At one with the moon and the sinking sun
At one with the softest breeze

Beyond the confines of infinity
Beyond the illusions of time

Beyond the powers of perception
Beyond human reason or rhyme

Perhaps when the journey has ended
And my spirit has flown wild and free
I'll rest in the depths of your wonder
At home with the stars ... you and me.

Preface- To-Day A Step Forward

[thoughts on retiring]

I wrote this poem in Sayulita, a tranquil piece of heaven on Mexico's Pacific coast where waters,mountains and jungle embrace in unison with angelic dark-eyed souls.Retiring from work after 44 years is a significant event worth celebrating. On February 2015 I sat by the breaking waves,margarita in one hand,pen in the other.In joyful disbelief I took a step forward as the words flew towards the calm of the turquoise seas.

To~Day A Step Forward

(thoughts on retiring)

The woes of the working class
And the dream of a distant dignity
Forty-five years
Since the child first leapt
Into the laborious dance of manhood
Today a step forward
Towards the soothing of a golden year
It's all over now Baby Blue
Dylan teasing the tangled moment
Today the unhurried breath
Beyond the authoritarian grasp
Beyond the regimental confines
Of a life 'tween nine to five

And the decency of an honest day
Drenched in the sweat of a workingman's blues
With life's constant companions
The enduring gifts of body and mind
Leaping through the motions
Of labour's daily rituals
Seconds into hours and it's time
Plodding home tired and strutting proud
Shillings in the pocket
Sigh beneath the weathered sky

Retired, rewired, rekindled, inspired
Aligned with the ease of a freebird's flight
There's a silence deep within the rising sun
A whispering through my veins
In the awakening hour the mystic
Unveils the morning mysteries
Today a step forward
Reflections on the journey's swiftfulness
The fiery tangents of time and toil
The vagrancies of the daily stampede
The ever encroaching twists of fate
And the pendulum's ceaseless crawling

Today the body rests
Today a sleeping serenity
Today a thought is cast
Towards the wild and warm awaiting winds.

Alaska 2000

Alaska 2000 is a travel journal relating a memorable period in my life. After 12 incredible years living in San Francicsco my wife Eileen & I bought an old Volkswagon van and pointed the wheels north towards Alaska. This was our final adventure before returning to live in Ireland and commencing our new life within the scenic beauty of the Wicklow Mountains.

Our journey was destined to be wild and wonderful. Alaska, the last frontier where men outnumber women and the ladies say "the odds are good but the goods are odd." Alaska, a land whose beauty awakened my senses and changed the course of everything in my life.

P.S. All incomprehensible nouns (e.g. Og-- the Irish word for young, junkyard angel, Renoirette) are merely terms of affection attributed to my lucky damsel.) The Nugget was our (destined for disaster) VW van.

"ALASKA 2000"

Friday 28ᵗʰ July.

    Yesterday my heart was burning and my feet had need to fly. We crossed the Golden Gate bridge at 1.30 p.m. Hendrix roaring Dylan. The moment was deliciously painful. My Og stole a final glance. Alas! The city was gone, draped in a white blanket, quietly invisible. The relished memories would have to suffice. A few tears evaporated within the fog. Heading north, two riders were escaping, the wind began to howl. Good-bye's too good a word babe, so I'll just say farethewell.

    Alaska bound, listened to the relieving silence of a redwood forest. Rested Nugget at Van Damme beach, kissed to the encore of a honeymoon, collapsed into a twelve hour series of dreams, momentarily interrupted by galloping foam. Manãna Mendocino.

San Francisco

Mendocino

Saturday 24ᵗʰ July.

The unspoilt jewel remains intact. Mendocino, ocean-hugged, wind swept, God touched. Your language is bird-song, your pendulum a swaying fern, your gardens all artist's palettes, your ever-changing sky, morning blue as a deep emotion, snow-balled with restful mid-day clouds, fiery with rapidly cascading afternoon fog, tranquil as midnight jewelry box silently sparkles in distant mysterious darkness.

During an afternoon hike along cliff-edged cavernous tide-pooled rock formations a warm souled elderly lady paused in our path. Upon observing, she kindly requested that I remind my wife how blessed she is with beauty. Finally she points her finger seaward towards my face and demands me to write down my thoughts every day. We all smiled contemplatively and bid the moment adieu.

Whilst slumbering in nearby Casper words were gently spoken and thoughts softly written.

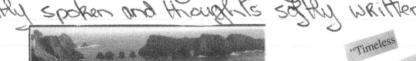

"Timeless Mendocino Coast"

Sunday 30th July.

Breakfast was a combination of simplicity and perfection, two aspirations for the remainder of my life. Our only companions were trees, silence and the awakening of dawn. My heartbeat slowed in response to such kindness.

Jughandle State Reserve is a geological treasure. The self-guided nature trail is aptly named "The Ecological Staircase." Our four mile hike commenced through a pine forest, advanced to breathtaking views of the Pacific coast, continued through a redwood forest and finally arrived at a uniquely rare pygmy forest. Soil deprived of iron and other nutrients due to heavy winter rains draining top-soil stunted the growth of these trees. Hence miniature cypress, huckleberry, Manzanita, Douglas Fir etc. Their ability to cling to life proved awe-inspiring.

With great excitement Og and myself proceeded along Rt. 101 towards the scene of my second marathon run, "Avenue of the Giants", majesty at its most indefinable. The adjacent Eel river offered us a wonderfully limb-soothing swim. Salmon, potatoes and the decadence of a wee Grand Marnier nightcap preceeded much needed folded eye.

Jughandle State Reserve

the **Ecological Staircase**

THE REDWOODS

Here, sown by the Creator's hand,
In serried ranks, the Redwoods stand;
No other clime is honored so,
No other lands their glory know.

The greatest of Earth's living forms,
Tall conquerors that laugh at storms;
Their challenge still unanswered rings,
Through fifty centuries of kings.

The nations that with them were young,
Rich empires, with their forts far-flung,
Lie buried now—their splendor gone;
But these proud monarchs still live on.

So shall they live, when ends our day,
When our crude citadels decay;
For brief the years allotted man,
But infinite perennials' span.

This is their temple, vaulted high,
And here we pause with reverent eye,
With silent tongue and awe-struck soul;
For here we sense life's proper goal;

To be like these, straight, true and fine,
To make our world, like theirs, a shrine,
Sink down, Oh, traveller, on your knees,
God stands before you in these trees.

Author: Joseph B. Strauss
Builder of the Golden Gate Bridge

Eel River

Banana Slug

MENDOCINO

AVENUE of the GIANTS

Monday 31ˢᵗ July.

Mosquitos forced a rapid exodus from Humboldt Hidden Springs campground. Proceeded at carefree pace along the 31 mile paved road through Avenue of the Giants. This gauntlet of antiquity dates B.C. and most definitely was created the very second God contemplated beauty.

The Founder's tree is dedicated to those whose turn of the century insight helped preserve redwoods from inevitable oblivion. It stands 346ft 1 inch tall with a circumference of 40 ft. To view this miracle Eileen and myself hiked through a pristine ancient redwood forest. The sun's beams highlighted dense beds of lady fern, sword fern and sorrel etc. Thousands of approximately 1,200 year old giants silently command respect whilst fallen monsters still retain integrity. This humbling experience is a gift to any life. Surely amongst these trees lies the dwelling place of our mother's most contented heart.

At dusk our resting spot was Prairie Creek State Park snuggled between roaring waves and sheer mountain edges echoing the ocean's music. At sunset four antlered Elk (huge stags) appeared grazing in a meadow within hearing distance. Our day of wonder reached completion. Darkness fell as the water's rhythm slumbered our consciousness.

Tuesday 1st August: We shared the verdant breakfast table with a herd of Elk. Ten eventful years have passed since we hiked the magnificent Fern canyon trail. With awe struck expectations we ventured down memory lane. Carved by a gently winding stream the canyon is approx. 200 feet high and 40 feet wide. From top to bottom its walls are majesticly adorned with lush green ferns constantly weeping from the mystical fog creeping down. Embroidered along the upper perimiter of the canyon rests the edge of the Redwood forest. Our early morning hike blessed us with solitude. The forest was totally ours. Every weaving curve and hilltop ascent unveiled yet another vision of wonder. Every fallen burl, mossy branch, crawling banana slug etc combined to paint the perfect canvas. Our advancing momentarily interrupted a resting deer who fleetfootedly vanished behind a billion emerald pines. Before returning to Ireland this Redwood experience will possibly be our last. The memories remain indellibly precious. We kissed and headed north with words unspoken. Oregon border farewell California, I glanced at the Óg's watery eyes. My heart is hers. Our new life officially begins. With her strenght and my dedication I fear not. True love knows no bounderies. Town of Brookings, parked Nugget 20 feet from vast Pacific, savoured a reviving swim, jogged 1 mile on beach. As the sun vanished, me and my shadow clinked two plastic glasses together, giggled and fed the veins a much needed dose of Möet Chandon.

Wednesday 2ⁿᵈ August

Continued north
along Oregon's magnificent
coastline. Everywhere smothered in densely
lush pine forest overlooking endless beaches. Sig-
-nificantly less populated than California. Long stretches of sand and
freeway totally empty. Truck loads of redwood trees are constant reminders of
the fragility of it all. Excluding lumber the Oregon economy is evidently clinging
to a lifeline. Minimum wage prevails. Towns are humbly adorned and sadly
unmemorable. However people remain kind spirited, helpful and smile
with ease. Those elusive moments when the heart is truly warmed must be
safely stored for recollection when
the winds of changes shift and life's harsh
unfoldings require soothing. To sub-
stitute the maddening haste associated with
city sophistication for the less prosperous
life of peace and quiet is our choice.
Mine is made.

Resting place for night at tree lined
lake on Umpqua Lighthouse State Park
Champers at ripples for sunset.

UMPQUA

Thursday 3rd August

Early morning is my favourite time to ink thoughts. Though conscious, life still seems to be emerging from slumber. I'm an island, pondering the notions that constantly float within the canyons of mind. Eileen's sketching a lake below the campground level. I'm alone, surrounded by graciously aged trees and birds whose early morning frivolity amuse my weariness. I'm so simply contented I wish time could freeze itself. Being aware that the remainder of my days will contain highs and lows, I pray that many more of these short lived blessings will accompany my journey. Time to roll wheels towards the unknown.

175 miles and halfway up the Oregon coast we veered inland parallel to the Umpqua River. Our destiny was the tranquil abode of the world's most indefinable brother-in-law. TJ's soul mate Nancy greeted us with heart warming hospitality. Her surroundings were idyllic. Acres of unspoilt pines, alders etc framed her beautiful shingled home. Bissy and Koko wagged their welcoming tales. Brice Creek provided our gypsy limbs with much needed rejuvenation. The master pipe blowing worm breeding chef arrived like a cool breeze and joined the family for a culinary extravaganza. As darting flames fled towards the crescent moon my eyes closed contentedly surrounded by a little piece of heaven.

From Nancy's garden

Friday 4th August

Myself, Og, Nancy, Sissy and Koko drove eight miles through winding woods. Zero traffic. Perfect afternoon swimming, resting, conversing. Beautiful rapid flowing mountain stream with 8 ft. deep sun drenched swimming hole. It's been a week since we crossed the Golden Gate bridge. In seven short days we've experienced places, people and lifestyles that instantly iradicate any notion of regret. San Francisco will always be a treasured part of our lives. Our little jewel became a concrete jungle. Leaving was difficult, looking back is easy.

My time leisured amongst Nancy's enchanting surroundings has filled me with optimism. The hours here provided an insightful preview into my future existence. Moving at the pace of a yawning petal must surely be the way man was conditioned to exist. Purposeful duties replacing a life of relentless haste. The mere thoughts of plucking my very own potato from love-touched soil excites me beyond description. The call to the wild has beckoned and my hearts whisperings offer no choice.

As darkness crept we chose to behave like children. Sleeping outdoors under an eighteen year old birch tree, glancing skyward in anticipation of a shooting star, giggling at the simplicity of it all. Eventually embraced as one, seduced into a world of dreams, the wings of reverie took flight.

OUR → blanket

Washington

Saturday 5ᵗʰ August.

To-day the activities between sunrise and sunset were almost perfectly motionless. Walked 300 yards to River's edge, got wet, gazed at rocks, got dry, gazed at trees, got wet, slept, got dry, burnt limbs, awoke, gazed at sky, headed home, savoured Hendrix, slept under blanket of birch tree.

← Blueberry

Sunday 6ᵗʰ August.

Early morning departure from the beautiful dogs and their blissfully docile owners. Drove 300 miles through northern Oregon. Mount Hood's breathtaking snow peaked vastness grasped all our senses as we crossed the ever raging Columbia river into Washington State. Pampered Eileen with grilled oysters in sleepy Chehalis. Highway 101 north into Olympic National Park. Finally Lake Quinault (on Indian Reservation), bordered by dense forest dramaticly shouldering eerie fog bank. Snow capped mountains in distant view. So far everywhere people have been politely quiet in campground environments. Perhaps excessive vociferousness is associated with city arrogance. With mother nature puppettering my heartbeat, life evidently flows gentler. Tequila and orange juice ten feet from view of leaping fish. Warmed by campfire. The best things in life are unquestionably free.

THE EVERGREEN STATE

LAKE QUINAULT

Rain Forest:

Monday 7ᵗʰ August.

Began day by hiking Quinault Rain Forest. Comparable in beauty to those Eileen and myself have explored in Belize and Hawaii. Saw huge Osprey nesting on top of Douglas Fir while sound of waterfall echoed soothingly.

QUINAULT RAIN FOREST

Monday August 7TH (CONTD.)

Following Rain Forest Hike we drove one hundred
miles through both Indian Reservation land and Olympic National
Park. Clear-cutting of forests by lumber companys is evident almost
everywhere, however the law requires replanting within four years.
So thankfully Oregon and Washington states are still blessed with
an abundance of beauty. An entire region's dependence on trees as
a source of livlihood is surely a recipe for both economic and
environmental disaster. Thought, energy and government
assistance must be given towards producing an alternative
job creating industry.

At 3 p.m. Og sighed as we feasted our eyes on this evening's
resting spot. Lake Crescent nestled at the foot of the 4,600 ft.
Sourdough mountain covered 100% from foot to summit with
emerald Douglas Firs. Swimming in the cool clear teal coloured
water beneath the descending sun gave my life a memory to
treasure. Eileen sketched the majestic scene before we returned to
set flames-a-flyin' and the Nugget-a-Rockin'.

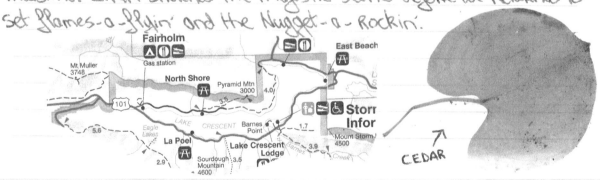

114

Tuesday 8TH August.

Converting the ordinary into the extraordinary, that's the purpose of plucking a solitary leaf, hiking endless trail after trail, gazing at the sky nightly, listening to a breeze, or looking deep into a stranger's eye.

To-day the streets remained motionless and our feet labouriously ventured towards unseen rims of land and water. Our physical capabilities were stretched to the limit by climbing 3 058 feet to the summit of Pyramid Mountain. The laborious effort was simultaneously joyous and painful. From the top our view of Crescent Lake was truly wonderous. Silent rippling silver saddles waltzing endlessly. The monsterous steep array of mountains seemingly emerging from the deep blue water complimented our view in breathtaking fashion. Our tired and sore limbs completed the descent at 3:30 p.m. Still in dense forest a sign pointing towards the lake simply said "picnic tables." We arrived at the pearly gates. The lake, 14 encroaching mountain peaks, the mid-day sun etc. all encircled our stunned vision. Ours and our alone. Smoked salmon sandwiches preceeded the water's revitalizing embrace. The moon slowly emerged as the sun vanished. Eileen's Johannisberg Riesling and my less pompous appetizer faded along with our graciously contented souls. A surprisingly simple day evolved into a memorable jewel.

LAKE CRESCENT

Wednesday 9th August.

Seven A.M. Lakeside. As the morning sun extracted smokey clouds, the forest appeared to be ablaze as a raging inferno. Yet total tranquility abounded as even the water's motion had still to awaken. Glaciers curved the precipitous valley within which this 600 foot lake was created. With regret, we departed en route to Bremington and boarded the car ferry to Seattle. The weather kindly provided a perfectly cool breeze for the scenic traverse of Puget Sound. Being first car on deck the Nugget provided a front row seat view as we approached terra firma. Van Heflin loudly bellowed as portside aimed directly at the famous "Space Needle" landmark. I pampered my junkyard angle with a water-view room at the Edgewater Hotel. Seattle is a pleasantly paced, sparsely populated city. Junky old architecture appealing to my wrinkled eye co-exist with shiny new monstrosities. Oddities include, railroad running through centre of town, Australian vintage electric trams, low flying planes directly overhead, all supplemented by the sanity of seagulls and boats everywhere. Rainy temperate climate comparable to Ireland. Very relaxed atmosphere. Lack of historical interest and notable landmarks slightly frustrating. Seattle's weekend backgarden includes the San Juan Islands, Vancouver Island and Olympia National Park. A haven for outdoor activities. Prevalence of book-shops and conversation-laden coffee houses indicates that Seattle's main attribute may indeed be the mentality of its amicable residents.

E

Hotel Edgewater

Thursday 10TH August.

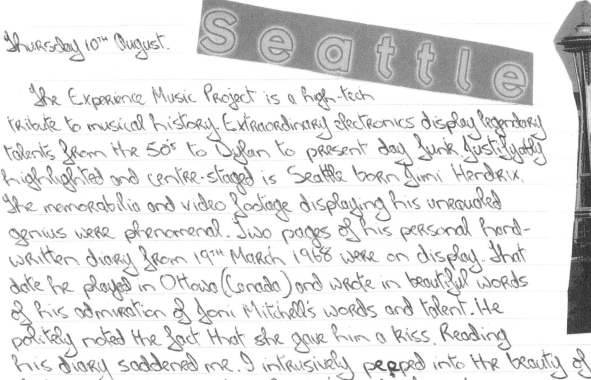

The Experience Music Project is a high-tech tribute to musical history. Extraordinary electronics display legendary talents from the 50's to Dylan to present day funk. Justifyably highlighted and centre-staged is Seattle born Jimi Hendrix. The memorabilia and video footage displaying his unequaled genius were phenomenal. Two pages of his personal hand-written diary from 19TH March 1968 were on display. That date he played in Ottawa (Canada) and wrote in beautiful words of his admiration of Joni Mitchell's words and talent. He politely noted the fact that she gave him a kiss. Reading his diary saddened me. I intrusively peeped into the beauty of what was and the wonder of what might have been.

Drove 70 miles from Seattle Camano Island State Park, a peaceful peninsula on the Saratoga passage.

Tomorrow, one hour north on Highway 5 and the beginning of a dream.

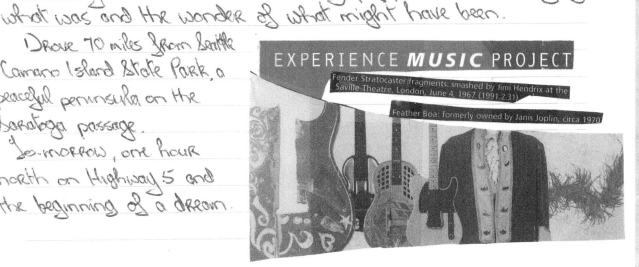

EXPERIENCE *MUSIC* PROJECT

Fender Stratocaster fragments: smashed by Jimi Hendrix at the Saville Theatre, London, June 4, 1967 (1991.2.31)

Feather Boa: formerly owned by Janis Joplin, circa 1970

Friday 11th August

Bellingham 2 p.m. On 22nd March '82 I dreamed of mountain-tops, life's road was a mystery, survival was a necessity, never an option, Miami's sand dunes offered comfort, I dreamed of music, clutching fishing nets from the Gulf of Mexico helped carve the dream, painting buildings in San Francisco helped carve the dream, a strengthened spirit helped carve the dream, a blue-eyed brunette coloured my dream. Falling snow filled my mind, distant horizons teased, empty pockets built strength, I sneered at adversity, music was a pay check away, failure was impossible, Steinbeck reminded me of that, Jack London whispered about that, Frederick Douglass dignified that, I told myself that. I missed music yet Zimmerman roared incessantly.

To-day arrived slowly, eighteen years can be a lifetime, the contents of mind can rage. Memories linger hauntingly. To-day a stillness, to-day a calmness, to-day the passions flow. To-day my boat sets sail. Life turns dramatically. Life is kind. It's okay to shed a tear. It's appropriate to smile. It's soothing to think. It's time for love and love only. Soon my blood will be swaying on the foam. The mountain top is in sight. Alaska's this side of Ireland. I'm looking at the boat pendulum like a heartbeat. My bags are full of music, it's all mine, four short hours, me and my grape filled sponge, blowin' in the wind.

Friday Aug 11th (cont'd)

Wheels rolled onto the MV MATANUSKA at 4.00 p.m. Our front deck, room with a view, instantly became a campsite. Organized chaos, tents, sleeping bags etc. everywhere. Everybody's face was fantasy-filled and overflowing with genuine excitement. The human diversity was beautiful. An instant family was created as acquaintances rapidly unfolded themselves. The horn sounded at 6.30 p.m. and the receding water foamed the vanishing shore. Eyes darted franticly as endless views emerged behind every island, mountain and nameless piece of land. The almost full moon haughtily floated as we steered past Vancouver. With the stars offering guidance my peachtree and myself found our way towards the goddamn saloon. Immediately our imbibing companions included a native Indian Alaskan lady, her Ozark mountain husband, an Aussie, unidentified souls and of course a Glasgowman intending to visit the Grand Canyon who somehow ended up on a slowboat to Alaska. The crack was brilliant. Alaskan Pale Ale beer kindly introduced itself to my long suffering intestines. Stepped outside, inhaled the sea, sky and distant lights, succumbed to slumber and lay within the darkness.

1 A.M. Eileen franticly wakes me and says two words, "Northern Lights." The rolling deck confirms I'm not dreaming. The Aurora Borealis. A celestial ballet. The sky bridal-veiled as God puppeteered the magic with indefinable sultryness. Ghost-

M.V. MATANUSKA

like waves of transperent snow flapped and weaved as the angels tossed their bed sheets within the astral wonderland. Angel wings danced in mystical disarray. Surrealism, impressionism, spiritualism all combined to momentarily transport my senses into untravelled territory. The nocturnal artist nonchalantly brush-stroked the diamond studded canvas teasing imagination. I'm surely floating in the abode of the Gods. Meteorites and shooting stars emit gasps of disbelief from everybody. Below, the sea mirrored the galaxy's magnificence. My entire experience was a powerful blessing. I slept in the womb of it all.

NORTHERN LIGHTS

ALASKA

Saturday
12th August

The MV Matanuska travels approximately 432 miles daily making the 946 mile journey from Bellingham to Juneau a 2½ day adventure. Sleeping on deck exposed to the elements assures that eyes open with the sun's rising. A more idyllic awakening is hardly possible. Through weary eyes almost everyone was discussing the Northern Lights. To-day we advanced through the narrow Queen Charlotte Strait. Everywhere the water's edge is tree line with pine forests. Snow capped peaks soar in distant view. The ship's restful calmness was suddenly interrupted by the welcome appearance of three beautiful humpback whales. Their black and white vastness protruded skywards before submerging leaving the spouted water misting across the waves.

5 p.m. Binoculars scanning aimlessly. Suddenly, yellow beak, snowy head, piercing eyes, gliding wings. The bald eagle, king of the blue jungle.

5.30 p.m. Salmon jumping, misty explosion, two more humpback whales. Alaska's welcoming committee resides in air and water.

6.00 p.m. Goddamn saloon, everyone already gargling. 10.00 p.m. Alaskan jokes, Irish jokes, bluegrass songs, Dublin's Fair City, last call, embracing comraderie, time to dream.

Sunday 13th August,

At 5.30 A.M. the sun peeped over the Misty Fjord ice peak. The cool Alaskan air filled my lungs as we disembarked at Ketchikan for a two hour stopover. With footprints in the sand I bowed and kissed the ground. Alaska, the very word shivers the pores of mind. Savagely pristine landscape. The added good fortune of beautiful weather has enhanced every moment aboard the Matanuska. Jimbo's of Ketchikan provided breakfast for our entire band of gypsies before we bid adieu.

Fortitude of mind I believe derives from the combined powers of love, spirituality, nature and the arts. The people of Alaska are strong minded and passionately attached to the powers of their unique surroundings. The challenge of surviving within extreme elements is regarded as a heavenly gift which generates self-esteem and intense depth of belief. Stoned on water, stoned on sky and stoned on all the heart-wrenching majesty in between.

Mid afternoon's placidity suddenly interrupted as leaping dolphins frolicked in their aquamarine home. Brief disembarkings at Wrangell and Petersburg before our final night's repose on a ship I'll love forever.

Wrangell, Alaska
The Inside Passage

Monday 14th August

Alaska's capital Juneau has no roads in or out. Access only by sea or air, a beautiful indication of the mentality. Our ship docked twelve miles south of town at 6.30 AM. We immediately grabbed a nearby campsite spot with glacier and lake view. Albert, the ship's bartender and Juneau resident had kindly offered us the opportunity of a dream adventure in his canoe. Mendenhall glacier is twelve miles long, 1½ miles wide with an average depth of 100 feet. Its varying shades of blue (dependant on density) are truly spectacular. The surrounding lake, river, mountains, waterfalls, mist and ever-changing meteorological conditions combine to make the view incomparably wonderous.

We hiked a short trail across the Mendenhall River. Huge sockeye salmon were spawning almost within arms length. Shortly after, Eileen's long anticipated moment arrived, her first bear sighting, brief yet wonderful. Her excitement was a joy to behold

We canoed the entire lake circling floating blue icebergs eventually docking on solid ground adjacent to the cavernous multi-alpined mountain of ice. Eileen and Albert savoured the view while I, with trepidation and surefootedness descended and climbed on top of the glacier itself. With respect, fear and an unprecedented level of anticipation I explored the majesty of it all. Suddenly a familiar soothing sound within the glacier, an ice-cave with flowing river of melted water. The grasp of passion offered no choice. I abandoned caution and entered a surreal world of blue light filled transparent ice. The endless stalignite-like peaks dripped their symphony into the rambling river. Light reflecting light exposed the depth of the shiny smooth dripping landscape - carving walls. The precious moment was mine, the memory indelibly etched. Our Creator's power touched deeply. I kissed the ice and slowly departed.

Mendenhall Glacier

MENDENHALL GLACIER
INSIDE PASSAGE
ALASKA

Tuesday 15th August.

Adventure travelling is always exhausting. Myself and my Marie Shelley slept in the arms of Morpheus for a solid twelve hours. By morning the physical recovery was complete. Rising mist uncurtained the glazier. The rain had vanished and my junkyard angel's nectarine pancakes revived the senses. Its 17 days since we left San Francisco, life is beautiful. Its 17 days since we worked, life is beautiful. Its 17 days since we escaped the clutches of conformity, the maddening 9 to 5, the increasingly senseless rat race. Life is beautiful. Our adventure will reach its epilog, our life's journey will steer towards its new beginning. Challenges will be embraced rather than feared. Right now all is a heavenly wave, Eliza is smiling with ease and laughing like thunder. My eyes are submerged in water.

The Mendenhall glacier is circumferenced by cloud-touching mountains steeply carved by the retrieving ice. To-day we hiked the eastern slope. The mountain's rain forest is densely coated in lush green moss. Ferns abound in drenched habitat reminiscent of another land I spent some time dwelling within. The elevated glacier views induced silent pondering. The concept of the beginning and end of everything searched my thoughts. I eagerly longed to return to the ice cave, the heart, the soul, the lotus, the lovely lonliness within. Peutétre mañana.

Wednesday 16th August.

Monday's ice cave experience impacted me like the scent of first love. The call of the wild demanded more. Without canoe, the only glacier access requires a death defying act of pure madness. The park ranger informed me of a secret route local Alaskan residents use. A vaguely identifiable trail weaves through bear habitat for the first two hours. Inevitably, for periods of time I was lost. Lairs of mountains lay between me and the thus far unseen glacier. I entered forest so dense no light offered guidance. By climbing over and bending branches I slowly advanced, eventually emerging upon solid mountain rock. My location markers were pink ribbons tied to twigs, store upon store and identifiable distant mountain curves. With great caution I'm suddenly rock climbing finger-clinging to ice-carved edges. I whispered a little prayer and advanced. Finally, another ascent and the slowly-advancing blue iced mountain fills my vision. The first cave entrance was arch shaped and somehow wonderously fearful. I advanced with extreme caution. My boots submerged in liquid muck before the secure relief of terra firma. The stunning view emerged instantaneously. A 400 foot arched tunnel of dripping blue ice. My breath echoed. I felt like the last human on earth. The river of melted ice-droplets slowly sauntered beneath. Its depth was a mystery I surefootedly would never unfold. No flies, only water, oxygen, light and a son of Dublin town. Any fear of ice collapsing or bears attacking was totally eradicated by the overpowering spirituality of the moment. Approx. 8 hours later, blistered feet and exhausted body eyed my blue eyed Eskimóg who greeted my safe return with hot Alaskan salmon and of course Schramsberg blanc de blancs Champagne.

Thursday 17ᵗʰ August.

Juneau is located in a picturesque valley nestled between ice field glacier laden mountains on one side and across the Gastineau Channel lies Douglass Island on the other. It's home to 30,000 Alaskans, Whites, 13% Tlingits (Native Indians) plus other ethnic diversity. Yes-day whilst strolling through the non-tourist perimiter I paused at the Evergreen Cemetery. An old tombstone embedded at the base of a huge tree grasped my attention. The inscription read "R. Dixon, Born 1819, Native of Ireland, 73 years old." Searching through the city museum's artifacts I discovered that Mr. Dixon arrived in Juneau by canoe eventually becoming the recorder of mining records and home owner. His courageous ability to circumspect half the globe at that era shivered my pores. His legacy touched my soul. With deep respect, his spirit moved me to have a beer (Alaskan Amber of course) in his honour. The Lucky Lady saloon adequately sufficed, accompanied by my "Dix-Sept" and Albert my favourite Alaskan bartender.

Yes-day was pleasurably endured recovering, relaxing and researching events for the forthcoming few days. Very un-Alaskan weather fortuiteously prevailed, blue skies and sunshine. As I write its 8.15 p.m., penultimite remnants of sun's rays seductively descend into another world leaving myself and my wee sponge very contentedly occupying space within the moon kissed lovliness.

JUNEAU

Friday 18th August.

We're travelling in an '86 Volkswagen Westphalia affectionately nicknamed "the Nugget." The only gold within lies stuck between my rear molars. The van is my rolling wheels, bed, restaurant, library, office, source of Bob Dylan's daily advice, comfort zone, sanctuary... and temperature plus inclination permitting the humble abode of Romanticism. Only an Irish condiment (or perhaps the odd Eskimo) could tolerate exposure at glacier level. I purchased the wheels last January in San Francisco, journeyed solo through Baja and Mexico, a memorable experience where the prison food was rather dubious. Like a woman's palm, a vehicle too can touch a man's heart. The "FOR SALE" sign hits the window next month in Anchorage. A little bit of my fragile heart shall vanish. It's time I revealed the truth. My purpose for carousing Eileen around Alaska is so next winter's weather in Ireland will not only be tolerable but possibly resemble the tropics.

Various nicknames I've attributed to my wife appear intermittently throughout this journal. For comprehension purposes please assume that any senselessly located noun is indeed a lovingly placed reference to my peachtree.

Friday 18th Aug (contd.)

I'm living in disbelief. Each day's wonderous unfoldings tend to improve on its predecessor. Thus far the aurora borealis and the ice caves stole the show. However to-day, in a three hour period I saw a bald eagle, a whale, dolphins, a bear and a moose.

We departed from Juneau aboard an Alaskan Marine highway boat en route to Gustavus. The eagle rested nonchalantly on a pole outside the ferry terminal. His eyes were piercingly contemplative. Advancing along the Gulf of Alaska the whale flapped its tail fin merely minutes before three dolphins joyfully played within the boats retreating white foam. Suddenly cruising parallel to a long sandy beach in the narrow stretch of water called the Icy Straits, a brown bear appeared roaming next to the breaking waves. His business-like enterprisings exuded an air of fearless authority. Finally, a bus transporting us within Gustavus braked hastily as a huge female moose avoided contact by inches before fleeing into lakeside foliage. My purpose for visiting Gustavus is to explore John Muir's discovery, the revered jewel call "Glacier Bay. To-morrow on board "the Spirit of Adventure" ship my "Queen of Everything" gets pampered once again.

GLACIER BAY
ALASKA

I'm glad you were here today
to see Glacier Bay & my family.

Esther Clark

Saturday 19TH August

Glacier Bay is a 55 mile long Y shaped passage of water
with numerous inlets and fjords fed and carved by the dozen or more
surrounding glaciers, nine of which continually deposit (calve) bergs
into the bay. These avalanches of ice constantly reconstruct the topography.
The spectacularly glaciated landscape is indeed the jewel of Alaska's
inside passage. It's bay is home to seals, otters, whales, porpoises etc,
while the shore homes birdlife, bears, mountain goats etc. The Thinglit
Indians call Glacier Bay their bread basket.

"The Spirit of Adventure" set sail at 8.00 A.M into misty damp
weather. The geographical and natural phenomenons I would experience
with the next eight hours will surely outlast most other contents
of memory. The Grand Pacific Glacier (the bay's oldest) has receeded
55 miles in 200 years, making it the fastest moving of all
documented glaciers. It's movement has revealed immense scientific
information since studies began with Scottish naturalist Muir

Sat. 19th Aug (contd.)

in 1879. Muir accompanied by hired Tlingit natives canoed from Wrangell to Glacier Bay in extreme Winter conditions. My already existant respect for his work, achievements and intellect is now accompanied by a new found awareness of his physical toughness

The brief crossing of water presented us with a huge array of outstanding memories; endless glaciers, snow-peaked mountain ranges, humpback whales migrating from Hawaii to Alaska, sea-otters, a lone black bear walking the sand, South Marble Island covered with birdlife including Tufted Puffins, Cormorants and Kittiwake gulls, Sea Lions, Grizzly bear, mother Grizzly bear with three cubs, Bald Eagles both nesting and on beach, plus endless unnamed sea-birds. To share a life's moment with one of these fellow animals is indeed a privilege. To share time and space with them all in one day amidst such breathtaking natural surroundings, is an honour beyond description

The glaciers, constantly calving, confettied the bay with thousands of bergs large and small. The inclement misty weather merely added to the mystique giving a sense of the creation of it all.

These lands and waters are Tlingit homeland. Retrieving ice forced their exodus. On board our vessel Wanda a native indian, beautifully presented a verbal and musical insight into their history and culture. Her aging mother emotionally accompanied three generations of their family incredibly marking the matriarch's first visit within these waters. She kindly commented in my journal.

I Humpback Whales

Sea otters care for their young and eat shellfish while floating on their backs.

Home of our Tlingit Ancestors

"And then the ice came. It was not just a white dot in the distance. It came fast. It knocked down all the houses. The people had to leave."

The colorful horned puffin.

Sunday 20th August.

The Alaska Highway begins seventy miles north of Juneau. Aboard the MV Malaspina we ventured slowly through the Lynn Canal before finally rolling the Nugget onto the road that rises towards the top of the world. This begins in the quiet yet strategicly located town of Haines, population 2,300. Surrounded by typical Alaskan splendour, this town has thankfully resisted the temptation to spoil it's beauty for the benefit of tourists. A sign on the closed fish market door basicly read "Owner next door." A pleasantly smiling lady conversing with her children nodded awareness of my minute dilemma. Almost ten minutes later her amicable demeanour arrives and a fresh Alaskan salmon was mine. Her ability to resist unnecessary haste or pressure is a blessing I wish to duplicate. Myself and my Renpirette have camped all over the western U.S. and parts of Canada. The campsite we acquired seven miles outside Haines is unquestionably our most beautiful ever. Sheer waterfall-laden mountains overlook the snake-like advance of the raging Chilkoot River. This salmon-filled songster feeds the aquamarine Chilkoot Lake. Beside this, the city-fleeing adventurers temporarily dwell. Following our Thai spiced rice and salmon-à-la-françois we decided to take a pre-dusk stroll along the rocky river. Fishermen's lines weaved and descended like an ocean's final leap. All was tranquil. Alas!, Alas!, Alaska... perhap's the

Sun. 20th Aug (contd.)

source of the beautiful name. Two grizzly bears emerge from within their verdant water-edged habitat. Our view was perfect, 150 yards on the opposite side of the river. Their appetizers were berry-filled bushes. Like mountains plucking pebbles they diligently savoured the delicacies. The main course followed. Submerged, swimming, their heads resembled floating islands. Fussily, they devoured only their favourite parts of the salmon. In total awe of the moment we followed their movements upstream for over an hour. Suddenly the largest brown bear stands totally upright, resembling a coastal redwood, he spies a fisherman and hastily vanishes within the mountain foliage. Straight above at tree-top level two bald eagles (they mate for life) patiently await the remnants of a ferocious feast. I'm beginning to understand why this icy land warms and steals the heart

. HAINES, ALASKA

Monday 21st August.

In the game of life, sunshine follows rain... literally. The stretch of the Alaskan Highway from Haines to Haines Junction is apparently the most scenic section. Low hanging clouds and torrential rain deprived us of views. Customs control at Canadian border almost passively non-existent. Briefly thereafter a sign "Welcome to the Yukon". Our only view was in the tourist guide book. Arrived at destination, clinked glasses in our mobile tavern and delved into sleeping bags with raindrops frolicking daintily.

Tuesday 22nd August.

6.30 A.M. Slapped lake water into dreary eyes. Rain headed east, wheels headed west. Alaskan blue cloud (i.e. fragment of sky) brightens our world. Eileen's musical choice, sultry jazz female mellows along with dawn's awakening. Suddenly our worst fear, the engine emits clouds of steam. The mechanic resembled a weather beaten gold prospector. He quickly deduced that the expansion plug (i.e. the equivalent of a bath tub stopper) had vanished draining the engine of coolant. German V.W. parts are as common in Burwash Yukon as Burmese hookers in the west coast of Ireland. He grabbed a handsaw, headed for the woods and emerged with a three inch twig which perfectly filled the hole. Yukon folk live off the land, a fact confirmed by the $35 twig. The Nugget advanced trepidly as the twig functioned admirably. However, with regular intervals the engine continued to overheat

Requiring roadside cooling off periods. One hundred stressful miles later we arrived at Beaver Creek, had a beer and decided to put our faith in the town's only mechanic whose show begins tomorrow morn at 8.A.M. Wednesday 23rd August. The birth of a nightmare. The nearest V.W. dealer is in Fairbanks. The Nugget is towed 320 miles across the Yukon, a $600 taxi journey. Our driver a 75 year old gentleman named Walt.

The Yukon stretches approx. 1000 miles, population 35,000 of whom 25,000 live in Whitehorse. Due to elevation and temperature extremes the land is predominantly covered with permafrost i.e. ice just below top-soil level. Trees barely survive. The landscape is wide open-spaced, barren and inhospitable. Discovery of gold in 1898 resulted in the construction of the highway and most of the adjoining towns. Mining is still the major industry in this wild lonesome terrain. Saw a moose and saw Fairbanks. One was beautiful, the other was a sadly despondent den of iniquity. Car news to-morrow,

Moose
Yukon • Alaska

Thursday 24TH August

"Gonna keep rollin' till the wheels fall off." Dylan's words say it all. My van, my wheels, my Nugget R.I.P. "You ain't goin' nowhere." Tis a solitary feeling to be motionless, miles from nowhere. The options are panic OR calmness. Available funds are suddenly very limited considering Ireland's half a globe away and selling the van was our financial safety net. Suddenly a town full of strangers represents my only guiding light. I seek honesty, compassion, good fortune and a few breaks. The weird truth is that there's something I find endearing about this sort of predicament. It gives the world a chance to be nice. I count life's other many blessings which render this problem rather insignificant. With time-earned optimism I await some source of human spirit to enter my path, seek my vision, say a few words, smile sincerely and solve my problem. Every problem has an inevitable solution, time is the only momentary interference. Small town mentality is kinder. Alaska epitomizes this reality. To-day was a chess game. Through a spider's web of inter-weaving connections, each step being the logical consequence of its predecessor, I sold a dead truck for a couple of grand green bills, rented a wife-pampering fancy set of wheels for half the acquired dough, plan to spend the other grand on a thatched-roof igloo in the North Pole. Surplus funds go on Yukon Arctic Red Amber Ale and the Champagne of my beachtrees choice. To-morrow will travel to gaze at America's highest mountain peak DENALI, meaning "the Great One." The sight will surely provide our tired hearts with a rejuvenating caress from the Mother source.

Friday 25th August.

To-day I hungered for retrieval of spirit-touching warmth. The initial seconds of a familiar piece of music can instantaneously replicate that feeling of relief. Fairbank's unfoldings challenged us. However, Alaska's pearly gate grasps the mind. Anticipation of nature's nurturing is a constant source of comfort. The last few days have bestowed unfortunate mishappenings. Our medicine is hope and patience. Seconds are teachers, hours are classrooms, days are lessons. All is purposeful. To-day I hunger for the love-scented all-engulfing peacefulness lying within the Mother's breast. I hunger for the feeling which has always been within mankind's grasp since the revolving globe first confused us. To-day the mountain-top, to-day "the great one", to-day DENALI.

Mt. McKinley, Denali National Park, ALASKA

Friday 25th (contd.)

Denali national park is over six million acres of alpine majesty. Indefinable wonder is everywhere. Year round snow covers hundreds of thousands of mountain peaks. All rivers are glacier-fed. Vast valleys of colourfull tundra extend beyond reach of the naked eye. Excluding the African plains, these valleys are home to as impressive array of wildlife that our world offers anywhere. Amazingly, for these animals their natural home is virtually untouched since its creation. One narrow dirt road winds through the park. Preservation of God's work has been a rare phenomenon. In 1917 legislation safe-guarded four million acres of this land. President Jimmy Carter extended this to six million in 1980. His wisdom and foresight will benefit our world forever.

We arrived at mid afternoon and immediately boarded an old bus which ventured 53 miles within this piece of heaven. We saw caribou, doll sheep, red fox, snow shoe hare, porcupine and a 1500lb antlered moose grazing between the colourful autumn foliage and snow covered mountains. The dominant spruce and birch help provide shelter for all creatures great and small. Sunset cast golden light on the land. Returning homeward a rapidly flying owl glanced, reminding us that life never rests in Denali.

Saturday 26TH August

America's highest mountain peak, located in the heart of Denali Park, is the 20,320 ft. Mount McKinley. Permanent snow fields exceeding 100ft. in depth cover more than 75% of this granite monster. Alas, due to clouds few visitors ever actually see this breathtaking spectacle. Today the elusive luck of the Irish prevailed, 99% cloudless blue sky, a rare occurance.

En route towards the mountain, the wide open terrain offered us a precious view of a mother grizzly bear and her two playful cubs. Oblivious to human interference their natural behaviour was a joy to behold. At a higher totally snow covered elevation a beautiful memory graced us. A solitary male brown bear trampling through his white canvassed terrain, rolling playfully down hilly slopes like a large free falling cascading rock. He eventually vanished over a hilltop leaving a trail of footprints as beautiful as any Renoir captured moment.

Mount McKinley denuded her elegance Dwarfing her encroaching neighbours she silently soared above all. At this sight surely the thoughtless must think and the dormant spirit must awaken itself. Teasingly the mere apex penetrated a solitary cloud. Pondering the unseen I left my footprints in the snow.

Sunday 27th August.

"To-day, peace of mind was soberingly relentless. The road was a grey brush stroke edged by autumn-leaved artist's palettes. The sky, varied shades of mingling hues constantly caressing the imagination. The placidity of the moment provided an opportunity to cast a notion. Extensive travelling is wonderful and indeed an education within itself. My romantic theory is that every warm beating heart seeks its own personal abode within our planet. The fortunate find Nirvana. Following my Alaska journey calculations lead me to the shelter of Irish mountains adjacent to Dublin's lovely heartbeat. Due to previous travel experiences, and assuming a lack of senility my heart's residence is dispersed partially in the jungles of Belize, the waters of Hawaii, the mountains of Canada, the bars of San Francisco, the deserts of Baja, the railroad tracks of Mexico and a small town in France. I'm destined for the eternal curse of always missing somewhere else. An element of lonliness will be my perennial companion. the grass will always be greener on the other side. Perhaps awareness of this fact is the foundation for dealing with the apparent problem. Perhaps the unworldly fool on the hill, the village idiot, is after all living the perfectly blessed existance. Perhaps my theory will prove itself fruitless. Perhaps I'll become the foolish idiot soaked in dancing raindrops and restful senility.

Sunday 27th August (contd.)

With reluctance we bid Denali farewell and headed south on Highway 3. I decided to search for some off the beaten track Alaskan town where the local community might share their words and philosophies. Our road led to Talkeetna fourteen miles east of the highway situated along the Susitna River. Our discovery proved to be a charming little jewel whose residents relish their simplistic lifestyle. Log cabins, snow mobiles, railroad tracks, rusty trucks, bearded mountainmen, crowded saloons, salmon burgers, two seater planes, friendly faces, friendly dogs and three young Irish woman living on the edge of town. The Rambling Cliffs joined us for a rake of gargle in the Fairview Inn saloon. Story telling and laughter extended until mid-night.

Monday 28th August. At 8.00 A.M. I was in the river beneath the railway bridge. Salmon were everywhere except on my hook. Jed, the kind hearted local gun swingin', moose hunting, bearded frontiersman befriended us and under his secure wing took Eileen and myself on a fabulous canoe fishing adventure on a spectacular lake hidden within the Talkeetna mountains.

143

Monday 28TH August (contd.)

Common denominators have resurrected themselves within the Alaskan persona. A passionate love of the land, an enduring acceptance of extreme climatic conditions, a strong self-esteem derived from surviving the elements, a need for sustinance fishing and hunting, a willing ability to actively contribute to the needs of their community, a strong awareness that the rest of the world is becoming increasingly hasty and senseless. A mere half million people are domiciled within this vast habitat. Doors are unlocked, crime is a non-entity. The "LAST FRONTIER" offers a lifestyle where the sacrifices are balanced against magnificent natural beauty and a peaceful pace of life virtually non-existent within most of our fragile mother. Most Alaskan residents are relocated non-natives. Such a dramatic move requires courage and tremendous spirit. Above all, these admirable qualities have grabbed my deepest respect. Within this land, the awareness that life's not a dress rehearsal is extremely evident. With greater frequency, Alaskans glance skyward, harmonize with the waters, talk to the animals, inhale the silence, laugh at their predicament, and wonder at the birth of it all. With envy I long to explore the canyons of the true Alaskan mind and bid adieu to the senseless raging forever sweeping across our emerald tapestry. For these reasons I awoke with the sun, seek the rising mist, long for the yell of wolves, and rest for a while 'neath the warm summer's sun. I sometimes tend to be equally exhilirated by a glance at the water's meanderings as by the smile of a stranger's eye. Alaska effortlessly provides an abundance of both.

Tuesday 29th August + Wed. 30th Aug

Kenai Peninsula

HOPE ALASKA

HOPE, population 200, twenty miles off the main road had irresistable credentials as for as my level of sanity was concerned. Three hours south of Talkeetna we entered the beautiful glacier-laden Kenai peninsula. When three cars resembled a traffic jam I veered right into the mountain's lush secrecy. Our rambling road endlessly advanced through scenic splendour until finally reaching the water's edge and the motionless intrigue of a town called Hope. Embraced by an arc of towering mountains this haven of solitude is the resting place for quite souls seeking serenity. A gold rush town, still proudly displaying charming architecture and turn of the century log cabins. The town's erivie silence merely enhances the astounding beauty of its natural surroundings. A classic century year old saloon is the only drinking establishment in town A wrinkly old rebel named Banjo poured my drink and proceeded to educate me in the delicate art of extracting a fish from water. This dubious task has so far proven to be beyond my primeval capablities. The evening fled deliriously. At sunrise, Banjo and myself alone in the wilderness, bordering the rapidly flowing six-mile river. His movements were precise and poetic epitomizing economy of effort. The man was at home in the wilds that famed the animal within. Before the cruelness of Alaska's hostile winter arrives, Banjo

Wednesday 30th Aug (contd.)

Will be self sufficient. His freezer will contain 50 salmon,
a moose and a black bear. All respectfully slaughtered for
sustinance. To-day between us we caught four silver salmon.
One of us caught none. Banjo ripped the branches off an
elder tree, struck a light, smoked and cocked a fish whose
final gesture still rippled the waters. Together we feasted,
two souls in harmony amidst the blissful loviness of it all.

Thursday 31st August.

        Due to my Queen of Everything's inherited dependence on
infrequent pampering our nights in Hope were comfortably
passed in riverside cabins with outdoor jacuzzi for imbibing
beneath the astral flickering. To-day our Hope-filled hearts advanced
along the winding miles. A few hours later we reached the town of
Seward, gateway to the Kenai Fjord National Park. Devistated by a
1964 earthquake, the recovering
economy's main attractions are
the numerous glaciers within
the park itself. A relatively
short hike took us to a glacier
edge. Beautiful yet diminutive
by comparison with others. He

DISCOVERY CABINS
Hope • Alaska

Proudly Operated by:
adventure
ALASKA

Thurs. 31ST Aug. (contd.)

town's main saloon depicts a gun swingin' frontier woman demanding whiskey and fresh horses for her men. Her audicious behaviour grabbed my "Blue Angels" approving eye. As darkness crept we headed for the woods and slept in our unloved rent-a-goddamn-car beside a nameless river. Without the nugget our comforts were greatly diminished and challenges arose, however Eileen's spirit soared accordingly to equal the task. At morning's emergence she hastily saunters arm-swinging towards the woods eventually re-emerging with branches and twigs heavily laden within her arms. Our spontaneous restaurant was the windswept coldness within our grasp. Within minutes flames were flying, tea was brewed and warmth was circulating within my veins. Generous portions of applesauce pancakes completed the banquet. She trampled dirt on the fading embers, spat, and nodded towards the road. I smiled a secret smile within, and sensed fresh horses would have appeared if my needs demanded. With hunger cared for we headed south. Our destination being 150 miles away where the road ends and the Gulf of Alaska pours its salmon into the Cook Inlet.

Kenai Fjords National Park

Fri. 1st + Sat. 2nd August.

Highway 1 south along the Sterling route offers an insight into several small Alaskan towns probably bypassed by most travellers. Exploring these backroads reveals each residence domiciled within wood sheltered solitude, an obvious prerequisite in a land where space is bountiful and the faint hearted have no desire to occupy. Surely this was how our Creator intended us to live before over population and a scent of greed re-directed our priorities.

Three hours later the road terminates, vanishing into sea drenched oblivion. A breathtaking backdrop of glaciers, mountains and seductive sea combine in stunning harmony to shelter and immaculately frame the land's-end town called Homer. A more spectacularly picturesque sight I've never seen, most surely the abode of the chosen few. Homer's livelihood is dependant on fishing especially halibut. Avid anglers journey from all corners to hook these white monsters which can weigh in excess of 300lbs A two mile narrow stretch of land called "the Spit" extends into the bay. A forest of fishing trawlers constantly crave for space creating Alaska's only traffic jam. The old wooden lighthouse still proudly casts it's beam across the foam however the building within is now the saw-dust floored "Salty Dawg Saloon". Fish stories prevail as sea-swept bearded bohemians hurl

(contd.)

Fearless glances through the rum-stained darkness. Outside a bronze commemorative statue honours their fallen comrades. Through the misty window pane I glanced as the glaciers blushed beneath the lowering sun, their melting ice invisibly cascading into the abode of fin flapping urchins. Oblivious to all, rusty faced fishermen cast bravado into the approaching stillness of an Alaskan night. Worldwide, the magnetism of a land's end has always seduced the gypsy soul. Their adventurous hearts are on fire, life is a death defying experience, the ocean is solid ground, befriending fear is a passive passion, and as the poet dreams of love, these hardy souls dream of the ocean's final frothy leap.

Sunday 3rd + Monday 4th August

When wheels must roll land's end offers one option. Leaving a warm embrace is always difficult. Alaska has both warmed and embraced. The moment to retrieve footsteps has arrived. Fortunately the airport is still a few moons away. ~~Both~~ Alone with ourselves, we slowly advanced with clutched memories, heading towards the other side of the world. Our future is as uncertain and fragile as the prayer of morn. Regardless, one glance towards the mountains conquers all fear within a mind blessed with love-touched rationality

(contd.)

Mountains empower the true Alaskan. They surrender their emotions to the whispering of the breeze. With defiant gallantry adversity is scorned. Having journeyed distances across this vast land I've observed a rare human phenomenon. Calmness, placidity, and inclination to smile with ease are human charact-eristics rampant throughout this sky-touching last frontier. Should my death-bed thoughts be granted an hour's recollection, my moments voyaged through this pristine wilderness will definitely accompany me until the journey's end.

To-day we hiked the upper trail of the Kenai river. Aqua-marine splendour silver-sandled beneath. Autumn colours contested for attention. With defenseless resistance we listened to our hearts and returned to the natural simplicity of a town called Hope. The entire single-digit populus acknowledged our return. A contemplative glance emerged from a friend called Banjo. We shared the evening then faretheewelled all. As campfire flames waltzed beneath the silence we filled hot-water bottles, checked for northern lights and dreamed of foreign lands.

HOMER, ALASKA

Hope, Alaska, at the mouth of Resurrection Creek
In spite of earthquakes, floods and the passage of time several
of the old buildings built about the turn of the century remain in
use on the main street of this historic mining town.

5TH + 6TH September

Since leaving San Francisco neither newspaper's words nor
television's sounds have intruded into my frame of thought. Today we
arrived in Anchorage. With relief the city actually presented itself as little
more than a quaint hospitable town. The concrete barely penetrated the
pores of mind. Alaska has 1.02 square miles of space per person. Its
largest city has 258,000 people, half the population approximately. Fine
museums and arts offer an insightful view into the State's history and
native culture. Recovering from pure exhaustion I choose to hang out
in the Side Street Espresso Café and Darwin's "Theory" pub while my
better half shopped ceaselessly for brown bear Christmas ornaments
and moose hot-water bottles. Our plane flies in 48 hours

ALASKA from SPACE

Any journey if worthwhile should render the traveller emotionally exhausted and with an altered state of mind. Knowledge previously assumed should be modified. Priorities should be re-prioritized. Former conclusions should be re-evaluated. The power to re-direct one's future should birth itself. To the attentive eye Alaska is a powerful educator. Courage is a derivitive of wisdom. To live here requires both attributes. For spiritual and physical survival the land offers everything. Alaskan land is different, more remote, more beautiful, more abundant, more extreme, more challenging and more rewarding. Everyday the eye is feasted and the soul nurtured. Genuine respect for all of nature's gifts is the fundemental foundation of all their beliefs. In winter daylight is reduced to mere minutes. The land is frozen. Simple tasks are arduous. Communities become extended families, a tradition inherited from native customs. With each plate of food the mind reflects on the source, gratitude overflows and the love of the land becomes deeper. From these experiences a spiritual fortitude paves the way for a life of inner contentment. These observances have rewarded my brief visit here with a deeper awareness of where love and freedom derive from. Next month myself and my Renairette will redirect our lives and move to

a tiny remote village in the Irish mountains. The land, the garden, the trees and the water will be our neighbourly companions. I believe my Alaskan memories will assist in warming cloudy days. Admittedly I'm slightly confused. I'm presently writing these words alone and in the middle of nowhere. A kind solemness lingers within my bones. My location is a sheltered valley within Alaska's Kenai peninsula. My eyes feast as melted glacier water is roaring, rolling and recorting admirably. I'm seated on a monstrous driftwood log, long since leafless yet still commanding admiration and respect. The valley's oval shaped all-encompassing blanket is fourteen white, green, grey and black mountain tops. The river curls ceaselessly yet evidence abounds that its width will soon quadruple. Winter snows are imminent, the skies will pour nourishment, the mountains will empty their chalices, drunken trees will scratch the heavens, banqueted bears will seek hibernation, pebbles will be smoother, mountains re-sculptured and a newborn butterfly will flutter frivolously within the ancient tapestry. All revolves, nothing really changes, the cycle of life merely sheds another pair of time.

Beside this river, as darkness looms, I'm alone, motionless as a rock, captivated by the power of a disappearing Alaskan stillness. Yet lonliness can never be a companion as long as passion's flame intoxicates and the spirit flows like the sound and sight of all around.

GLOSSARY

1. **Rosaleen**; Dark Rosaleen is a poetic reference to Ireland.
2. **Seanchai**; Traditional Irish storyteller.
3. **Liberties**; Dublin's oldest neighbourhood.
4. **Woodbines**; Cigarettes
5. **St. James' Gate**; Home of the Guinness brewery.
6. **Bewley's**; Old coffee shop on Dublin's Grafton St.
7. **Anna Livia**; Mythological name for Dublin's river Liffey.
8. **Silsean**; Mountain at foothills of Ballyknockan.
9. **Goolies**; Private parts
10. **Behan, Joyce, Wilde, Shaw**; Dublin writers.
11. **Buttercrust pan**; Dublin bread.
12. **Luke Kelly, Ronnie Drew, Phil Lynott**; Dublin musicians.
13. **Nelson's pillar**; Dublin monument blown up by the IRA in 1966.
14. **Lugnaquilla, Moanbane etc.**; Wicklow mountain names
15. **Glendalough** 6th century St. Kevin's monastic site.

Lightning Source UK Ltd.
Milton Keynes UK
UKOW07f0541080915

258258UK00001B/5/P